SOCIAL JUSTICE
GOES
TO
CHURCH

Jou Yaru
DEC 2020

"Jon Harris' excellent study shows how and when the current social justice movement found its way into the evangelical church. Along the way, he reveals a stark reality—that social justice in its spiritualized form 'parrots' the gospel message, positioning itself not as a 'gospel accessory' but as a 'gospel competitor.' The infusion of social justice into the gospel may well be the most dangerous problem facing the church today. Yet, it is going unnoticed in far too many circles. *Social Justice Goes to Church* can serve as a wake-up call exposing this most deceptive interloper."

—SAMUEL C. SMITH, PH.D.
Chair and Graduate Program Director
Department of History
Liberty University

"The great injunction to the Church was to preach the Gospel to the world, while not being of the world. Social justice neatly reverses this trend, preaching the ways of the world into the church. That is not its only critical reversal. The Gospel is about freedom from guilt and sin and bondage. Social justice seeks above all to apportion guilt and sin and bondage, enslaving entire demographics and requiring that they kneel before man in attrition. How important that a book of this nature should enter the fray right now. I applaud Mr. Harris for his excellent work in providing the practical means of identifying and repelling this fraudulent force, this ideological interloper, this dangerous false teaching."

—DOUGLAS KRUGER
Author of *Political Correctness Does More Harm Than Good: How to Identify, Debunk, and Dismantle Dangerous Ideas*

SOCIAL JUSTICE
GOES TO CHURCH

THE NEW LEFT IN MODERN AMERICAN EVANGELICALISM

JON HARRIS

Ambassador International
GREENVILLE, SOUTH CAROLINA & BELFAST, NORTHERN IRELAND

www.ambassador-international.com

Social Justice Goes to Church

The New Left in Modern American Evangelicalism

ISBN: 978-1-64960-080-6
eISBN: 978-1-64960-091-2

Cover Design and Interior Typesetting by Hannah Nichols
eBook Conversion by Anna Riebe Raats

AMBASSADOR INTERNATIONAL
Emerald House
411 University Ridge, Suite B14
Greenville, SC 29601, USA
www.ambassador-international.com

AMBASSADOR BOOKS
The Mount
2 Woodstock Link
Belfast, BT6 8DD, Northern Ireland, UK
www.ambassadormedia.co.uk

The colophon is a trademark of Ambassador, a Christian publishing company.

To Kenny Steier, a faithful friend. Until we meet again and hike the heights of heaven.

CONTENTS

FOREWORD

AT THIS MOMENT IN AMERICAN history, the Church has become overwhelmingly overrun with a parasitic false gospel of social justice. The very Christian faith that once gave birth to Western Civilization has been infiltrated and is, even now, collapsing under the weight of the parasite. Jon Harris' focus upon the pivotal 1970s era progressives brings great clarity to those wondering about the correlation between the political deconstruction of Americanism and corresponding usurpation of the authentic Gospel of Jesus Christ through the counterfeit of the progressive "Social Justice gospel."

Unlike the author, I am not a trained historian. I am a minister of the Gospel who has accepted a grace from above to interpret the world I now live in with the light of His inerrant and sufficient Scriptures. At the time of this writing, I can say with reasonable authority that the once beautiful Afghan Hound (modern Christianity) is not quite dead, but it is certainly emaciated, sickly, and lying on the ground in terrific jeopardy. With the turning of every page, Jon Harris will skillfully show you how this all came to be.

It is my prayer that the vitally important contents of Jon's excellent analysis will inspire the old hound to let out one last faith-filled howl—a cry loud enough to summon the attention of the Merciful Master. If the Merciful Master does not intervene, my dear reader, then the hound is as good as dead. We can still repent and retreat from Marxism, humanism, hedonism, secularism, socialism, and communism. We can return to a nation of individuals who practice the discipline of self-government under the everlasting authority of the Ten Commandments, empowered by grace from on High. My sincere thanks to Jon Harris for the careful retelling of this heretofore untold drama of American history. I commend it to your reading.

—Rev. Cary Gordon

Sioux City, Iowa

July 24, 2020

PREFACE

HISTORICAL SURVEYS OF AMERICAN EVANGELICALISM in general, and post-WWII evangelicalism in particular, tend to overlook significant contributions made by 1970s-era progressives who helped introduce the movement to New Left critiques of American culture. In a certain respect, this is understandable. Since the formation of the religious right in the 1980s, the reputation of evangelicals, in the greater culture, has largely been associated with political conservatism. The evangelical left temporarily appeared as a flash in a pan during the early 1970s, with fringe elements remaining through the 2000s.

Yet, fifty years after progressive seeds were sewn, their fruit has grown into a tree within the soil of modern mainstream evangelicalism. Institutional evangelical responses to political situations, such as efforts to normalize homosexuality, provide a path to citizen benefits for foreign migrants, accept government restrictions during the Covid-19 quarantine, support Black Lives Matter, etc. mirror the same kind of responses given by elderly veterans of the first progressive evangelical push. Yet, the pioneers of the movement have received little attention.

Between 1980 and 1991, during the height of the religious right's influence, historian George Marsden published three books on fundamentalism and evangelicalism, including *Fundamentalism and American Culture: The Shaping of Twentieth-Century Evangelicalism, 1870–1925*. Historian Mark Noll likewise contributed to a number of related books during the same period culminating in *The Scandal of the Evangelical Mind (1994).*

Both Noll and Marsden associated post-World War II evangelicalism with Fundamentalism, which they conceived as a version of American Christianity shaped by Scottish common sense realism, individualism, pietism, and dispensationalism, in reaction to higher criticism, Darwinism, and the social gospel. The parallel between Fundamentalism's anti-Communist tendency and the religious right's taste for smaller government made weaving a narrative of continuity logical and possible.

Noll mentioned progressive evangelicals like Ron Sider and Richard Mouw only in passing as ambassadors for introducing evangelicalism to Anabaptist and Dutch Reformed thinking.[1] In books like, *The Search for Christian America* (1983), Christian historians Marsden, Noll, and Nathan Hatch, criticized Fundamentalist-influenced evangelicalism for its characteristically populist anti-intellectualism and nationalism.[2] The culturally influential evangelicals worth writing about happened to be political conservatives.

Both Francis Fitzgerald and Steven Miller wrote extensive surveys of evangelicalism in recent years. In addition to covering Fundamentalism and neo-evangelicalism, their analysis also includes holiness and reformed traditions. However, in focusing on how evangelicals relate to the broader culture, they both emphasized conservative politics. In *The Evangelicals: The Struggle to Shape America* (2017), Fitzgerald briefly mentioned the "early 1970s . . . northern evangelical left" as "scholars" who came from "the Christian Reformed Church" and "Anabaptist sects."[3] Miller described "progressive evangelicals," in

---

1 Mark Noll, *The Scandal of the Evangelical Mind* (Wm. B. Eerdmans Publishing, 1994), 323-324.

2 The authors explain the religious right as a reaction to "the Supreme Court on abortion and the Bicentennial reminder of the Christian past" which "led to a new evangelical engagement in public life and fueled actions that were already underway." Their concern was both historical and practical. "The nature of culture shows that the idea of a 'Christian nation' is a very ambiguous concept which is usually harmful to effective Christian action in society." See Mark Noll, Nathan Hatch, and George Marsden, *The Search for Christian America.* (Crossway Books, 1983), 14, 17.

3 Francis FitzGerald, *The Evangelicals: The Struggle to Shape America* (Simon & Schuster,

The Age of Evangelicalism: America's Born-Again Years (2014), as failures having "few political victories to show for their efforts," with a "history" culminating in "tragic interpretation."[4]

H. B. Cavalcanti's book *Gloryland: Christian Suburbia, Christian Nation* (2007) downplayed the religious left by portraying post-World War II evangelicalism as a movement embracing modernity and the Republican Party. Almost since its inception, a continuous stream of books have created a genre of popular literature devoted to defining, and usually critiquing, the religious right.[5] This interpretation is consistent with the way evangelicals are typically depicted in the major media for their continuous support of Republican candidates. However, there were some exceptions.

Works such as Preston Shires' *Hippies of the Religious Right* (2007) and Darryl Hart's *From Billy Graham to Sarah Palin: Evangelicals and the Betrayal of American Conservatism* (2011) broke the mold. Shires located key aspects of the 1960s counterculture which made their way into mainstream evangelicalism and merged to form an unconventional Christianity. Hart believed evangelicals were underdeveloped politically and open to arguments from both sides of the aisle on key issues, though their instincts tended toward conservatism. Progressive evangelicals factored prominently into Hart's narrative. While neither author focused exclusively on the evangelical left, they did welcome them into the broader evangelical world without ignoring them or banishing them to the periphery. This kind of analysis was more common before the rise of the religious right.

2017), 251.

4 Steven Miller, *The Age of Evangelicalism: America's Born-Again Years* (Oxford University Press, 2014), 38.

5 Books in this genre: *The New Christian Right Mobilization and Legitimation* by Robert Liebman and Robert Wuthnow (1983), *With God On Our Side* (1996) by William Martin, *Onward Christian Soldiers? The Religious Right In American Politics* (1996) by Clyde Wilcox, *Jesus Is Not a Republican: The Religious Right's War on America* (2005) by Clint Willis and Nate Hardcastle, *American Fascists: The Christian Right and the War On America* (2007) by Chris Hedges, *God's Right Hand: How Jerry Falwell Made God a Republican and Baptized the American Right* (2012) by Michael Sean Winters, *Jesus and John Wayne: How White Evangelicals Corrupted a Faith and Fractured a Nation* (2020) by Kristin Kobes Du Mez.

In the 1974 book *The Young Evangelicals: Revolution in Orthodoxy*, Richard Quebedeaux characterized three generations of evangelicals using the labels "neo-evangelicalism," "new evangelicalism," and "Young Evangelicals." Neo-evangelicals emerged in the 1940s holding to "Orthodoxy but at the same time" repudiating "the theological and cultural excesses of Fundamentalism." The New Evangelicals softened their stance on inerrancy and dispensationalism, focused more on practical living, embraced social action, and dialogued with other religions, including Marxism. The "Young Evangelicals" took an extra step, prioritizing practice over doctrine by making practical living and social action the hallmarks of their movement.[6] Quebedeaux's "Young Evangelical" category entailed much of the original progressive evangelical movement. He believed, before the rise of the religious right, that evangelicalism was trending left both theologically and politically. As a contemporary observer his analysis was incomplete. Since then, others have more directly examined the topic.

Craig Gay devoted the first chapter in his book, *With Liberty and Justice for Whom?* (1991), to the evangelical left's opposition to capitalism. Gay proposed that there was "more going on within [the capitalism] debate than theological wrangling." Instead, "the conflict within evangelicalism appear[ed] to mirror a larger secular disagreement over social and economic policy."[7] Gay proposed that progressive evangelicals Christianized "New Left . . . social and historical analysis" in order to support anti-capitalism within Christianity.[8]

Despite the way most historians and sociologists overlooked or down-played the contributions of progressive evangelicals, their movement started to receive attention almost forty years later. David Swartz's *Moral Minority: The Evangelical Left in an Age of Conservatism* (2012) and Brantley Gasaway's *Progressive Evangelicals and the Pursuit of Social Justice* (2014), both presented a positive examination of progressive evangelicalism.

---

6 Richard Quebedeaux, *The Young Evangelicals: Revolution in Orthodoxy*, (Harper &Row, 1974), 3, 39-40

7 Craig Gay, *With Liberty and Justice for Whom?: The Recent Evangelical Debate Over Capitalism* (W.B. Eerdmans Publishing Company, 1991), 2.

8 Ibid., 56.

Swartz provided an excellent survey of biographical and corresponding thematic material in order to give a full picture of the movement primarily from the 1960s through the 1980s. Swartz's strength lay in a copious amount of primary sources, including many from physical archives. Inaccuracies exist, but overall he chronicled well "the rise, decline, and legacy of the evangelical left."[9] Swartz did not philosophically engage the material, but Brantley Gasaway did.

Gasaway's survey of the evangelical left was arranged more ideologically. He examined progressive evangelicalism's root ethical origins and assumptions on issues like racism, feminism, abortion, sexuality, poverty, and war. Underlying the movement's positions is a public theology inspired mainly by "New Left," "Anabaptist," and "Catholic social teaching."[10] Concepts such as, "the common good," "substantive equality," and "pluralism" set the movement apart from their rivals on the Religious Right.[11]

This work aims to carry the examination further by tracing how progressive evangelicals justified their New Left thinking within the broader tradition of American evangelicalism. The scope of the study mainly focuses on the origin of the movement in the 1970s. Part 1, "New Left Radicals," introduces prominent founding figures of the early evangelical left, including biographies of their early years, and analysis of their collective crowning achievement: the Chicago Declaration. Part 2, "An Altered Orthodoxy,"

---

9 David Swartz, *Moral Minority: The Evangelical Left in an Age of Conservatism* (University of Pennsylvania Press, 2012), 3; In a chapter on John F. Alexander, Swartz states, "The new activist voices of Pannell, Skinner, Perkins, and Alexander made especially deep inroads within InterVarsity Christian Fellowship." However, the president of InterVarsity from 1964 to 1981 was John W. Alexander, not John F. Alexander. See Swartz, *Moral Minority*, 34 and "Remembering Pioneers," InterVarsity, May 10, 2002, https://intervarsity.org/news/remembering-pioneers; In a discussion on the impact of New Left sources on the *Post-Americans*, Swartz cites an article by Jim Wallis entitled, "Invisible Empire," in the November-December 1973 issue of the *Post-American*. However, no such article exists in that issue. Another article by Boyd Reese entitled "America's Empire," does cite New Left sources. See Swartz, *Moral Minority*, 58, 287 and "November-December 1973," *Sojourners*, November 1, 1973, https://sojo.net/magazine/november-december-1973.

10 Brantley Gasaway, *Progressive Evangelicals and the Pursuit of Social Justice*, (University of North Carolina Press, 2014) 37, 43, 60.

11 Ibid., 53, 62, 69.

surveys some of the hallmarks which characterized progressive evangelical theology such as their conception of the nature of salvation and the church. Part 3, "American Revival," analyzes the evangelical left within the historical context of neo-evangelicalism, Fundamentalism, and Revivalism. Far from completely breaking the mold of their parents and grandparents, progressive evangelicals preserved key traits of the historical trajectory preceding them. The conclusion, "The Fall and Rise of the Evangelical Left," analyzes the successful impact progressive evangelicals eventually had on mainstream evangelicalism. The terms "progressive evangelicals," "young evangelicals," and "evangelical left" are used interchangeably to denote the group of evangelical Christians motivated to organize on behalf of a commonly shared New Left critique of American society during the 1960s and 1970s.

PART ONE

NEW LEFT RADICALS

THE BIOGRAPHIES OF MOST LEADERS in the evangelical left follow a similar pattern. After experiencing a conservative upbringing in a
Fundamentalist or evangelical home, they were exposed to New Left ideas,
usually in college. After coming to a new understanding of the disparities
and injustices surrounding them, these young evangelicals became critical
of their culture, including their faith tradition. Often a crisis of faith, or
temporary rejection of Christianity, ensued. But, eventually they returned
to Christianity bringing with them their newly discovered New Left ethical
assumptions. Finally, they formed a new synthesis by integrating these ideas
with evangelicalism.[1]

Before involving themselves in political causes, Jim Wallis, William
Pannell, Tom Skinner, and Sharon Gallagher were all members of
Fundamentalist Plymouth Brethren congregations. John Alexander was a
pastor's son in the General Association of Regular Baptists. Richard Mouw,
a covenant child in the Reformed Church, grew up attending summer Bible
camps and reading "Moody Bible Institute devotional guides" before walking
forward at Madison Square Garden to the voice of Billy Graham. Ron Sider
carried, along with his rural roots, the memories of his family's membership

---

1 Craig Gay observed, "Many of those on the evangelical left" had "been raised in Christian
traditions, they became involved in the New Left during the 1960s and 1970s and then
returned to their traditions to attempt to integrate the radical social agenda of the New
Left back into them." See Gay, *With Liberty and Justice for Whom?*, 55.

at a strict Sabbatarian Brethren in Christ church.[2] Wes Granberg-Michaelson's rearing included membership at an "independent, Bible-believing" church, attending a Young Life summer camp, and living with the expectation that he would go to the family college: Wheaton.[3]

However, after completing their progressive journey, many of these former members of conservative Christian households could say along with Jim Wallis and Wes Granberg-Michaelson, "The evangelical subculture in which I was raised was infiltrated by pernicious racism, captured by right-wing nationalism, absorbed with rampant materialism, and defended by haughty self-righteousness. But it taught me to ask the right question. What about Jesus?"[4] For these emerging young evangelicals, it was necessary to rescue Christianity from enslavement to the corrupting influence of evil cultural forces the New Left had warned them about. Yet, they recognized the ultimate answer to society's maladies was not a secular revolutionary or Marxist philosophy, but a renewed understanding of Jesus and Christianity. Their belief in an equality which called for the elimination of disparities, overturning of hierarchies, and redistribution of resources could be achieved through a uniquely Christian social action plan.[5]

---

2 Swartz, *Moral Minority,* 33, 49, 89, 154.
3 Wess Granberg-Michaelson, *Unexpected Destinations: An Evangelical Pilgrimage to World Christianity* (Eerdmans Publishing Company, 2011), loc 402, 506, 574, Kindle.
4 Ibid., loc 62-63.
5 Commenting on progressive evangelical groups from the 1970s, Craig Gay wrote, "The analysis of capitalism, the cultural diagnosis, the advocacy of an adversarial stance against the status quo, the emphases on grass-roots political organization and 'community,' the advocacy of identification with the poor and oppressed, and even the emphasis on voluntary poverty are all secular New Left themes." See Gay, *With Liberty and Justice for Whom?*, 55.

CHAPTER ONE

JIM WALLIS

JIM WALLIS PRESENTED THIS "VISION" for "social liberation" in his 1976 book *Agenda for Biblical People*.[1] The editors at *Christianity Today* introduced the work by quoting a few "representative" lines:

> 'Biblical faith is subversive.' 'The people of the nonindustrial world are poor because we are rich.' 'The God of the Bible is clearly and emphatically on the side of the poor, the exploited, and the victimized.' 'The lordship of Christ over all of human life and affairs . . . is not only a personal but a structural and political fact of reality.' The church of Jesus Christ is at war with the systems of the world, not detente, ceasefire, or peaceful coexistence, but at war.'

The editor observed that Wallis blended "insights from the politics of the left with the concerns of those involved in charismatic, communal lifestyles."[2] His influences included thinkers from many quarters of a broadly Christian spectrum including neo-orthodox voices such as Dietrich Bonhoeffer and Karl Barth, social activists like William Stringfellow and Martin Luther King Jr., Jacques Ellul, a Marxist influenced Christian existentialist, Reformed theologian Hendrikus Berkhof, Anabaptist John Howard Yoder, Catholic intellectual Thomas Merton, quasi liberation theologians like Jürgen Moltmann and Rene Padilla, and a Southern Baptist trained

1 Jim Wallis, *Agenda for Biblical People* (Harper & Row, 1976), 8.
2 "Book Briefs: July 29, 1977," *Christianity Today*, July 29, 1977.

commune leader, Clarence Jordan.[3] Wallis wrote that the "most important distinctions in theology are no longer between high church and low church, evangelicals and ecumenicals, Protestants and Catholics, [or] Calvinists and Arminians . . . " but rather between supporters of "establishment Christianity" and practitioners "of biblical faith."[4]

Wallis discovered the biblical faith while reading "the biblical narratives with fresh eyes" after involvement in "the radical student movement."[5] Despite having undergone a "'conversion' as a six-year-old" he "began to see the wholeness and dynamic power of the gospel for the first time" only after leaving "church, family, and friends" to search for "countercultural alternatives."[6]

His journey toward the counter culture started during his teenage years. Books such as the *Autobiography of Malcom X, Crisis in Black and White, Hiroshima*, and *My Friend, the Enemy*, all contributed to forming a "commitment to the struggle for racial equality."[7] His "radical" high school English teacher Mrs. Wallendorf had a profound "effect" on Wallis as a young man, as did "listening to the black experience" in poverty-stricken and segregated Detroit.[8] However, it was Vietnam that "completed" his "alienation from the church."[9]

Wallis' thinking was further shaped at Michigan State University. He was deeply influenced by Arnold Toynbee's *America and World Revolution*, which argued that America's "world-wide anti-revolutionary movement in defense of vested interests" was similar to Roman Imperialism.[10] Wallis and his friends spent much time studying the political situation in Vietnam. They attempted to penetrate behind the lies of the American government and

---

3 "Ellul, Bonhoeffer, Yoder, Stringfellow, Berrigan, Moltmann, Merton, Martin Luther King, Gordon Cosby, Karl Barth, Clarence Jordan, Rene Padilla; [and] Hendrik Berkhof's book Christ and the Powers" were all cited as "standard bookshelf holdings of 'young evangelicals.'" See "Book Briefs: July 29, 1977."
4 Wallis, *Agenda for Biblical People*, 1.
5 Ibid., x, 13.
6 Ibid., ix, x.
7 Jim Wallis, *The New Radical* (Lion Publishing, 1983), 34-36.
8 Ibid., 36, 41.
9 Ibid., 47.
10 Ibid., 61.

discover the real reasons for war. "We had made the mistake of believing in America," Wallis wrote.[11] America, they came to discover, was like "former colonial powers . . . backed by wealthy elites" and really no different morally than "communist Russia."[12]

Wallis joined Students for a Democratic Society and organized protests at MSU. During the national student strike in 1970, Wallis, an elected strike leader, led "a couple hundred students" at night to occupy the student union building where they would set up an anti-Vietnam teach-in the following day. However, that day never came. Police raided the building and arrested everyone inside that night.[13] A similar event took place when Wallis and his friends tried to occupy the ROTC building. On that occasion, police used "canisters of tear gas" to dispel the crowd.[14] He was arrested numerous times for such activities.[15] Thinking back years later on this period of his life, Wallis admitted to being both a "radical student" and a "Marxist" before rediscovering his Christian faith.[16]

While Wallis found the "Marxist analysis" to be "attractive" and representing "the best idealism of our time," he did not believe it generated "enough vision or resources for spiritual and political transformation." He became "disillusioned with the patronizing and arrogant attitudes of left-wing ideologues." Wallis concluded that "capitalists exploit the poor, but the communists use their oppression as a means for power." He realized that the "violence," "manipulation of power," and "sexual . . . exploitation mirrored the system" they "were fighting."[17] It was time for something new.

---

11 Ibid., 53.

12 Jim Wallis, *Revive Us Again: A Sojourner's Story* (Abingdon Press, 1983), 52.

13 Ibid., 54.

14 Wallis, *The New Radical*, 50, 56.

15 Dan Gilgoff, "Evangelical Minister Jim Wallis Is in Demand in Obama's Washington," *US News & World Report*, March 31, 2009, https://www.usnews.com/news/religion/articles/2009/03/31/evangelical-minister-jim-wallis-is-in-demand-in-obamas-washington.

16 Tom Allison, "Beck Distorts Wallis' Comments to Claim He Is a 'Marxist,'" *Media Matters for America*, March 24, 2010, https://www.mediamatters.org/glenn-beck/beck-distorts-wallis-comments-claim-he-marxist.

17 Wallis, *The New Radical*, 69.

As a result, Wallis started reading the New Testament again and happened upon his "conversion passage" in Matthew 25 where Jesus stated, "as you did it to one of the least of these my [brothers and sisters], you did it to me." He then realized that God "had taken up residence among the poor, oppressed, the outcasts" and thus found in the person of Jesus an ethic for political engagement.[18] This development changed the course of his life. In 1970, he took his radical ideas with him to Trinity Evangelical Divinity School.

Wallis quickly became the leader of the "Bannockburn 7," a group of students who met regularly to "discuss the relationship of their faith to political issues, particularly the Vietnam War." The group circulated antiwar leaflets, organized a "free university" public forum, led a sit-in, and hosted "God parties." In 1971, they published the first edition of the *Post-American*, their very own social and political magazine. The front cover pictured Jesus with a crown of thorns and wrapped in an American flag. In addition to Christian sources, many articles in the *Post-American* drew from New Left thinkers such as Carl Oglesby, Gabriel Kolko, John Gerrassi, William Domhoff, Ferdinand Lundberg, C. Wright Mills, Richard Barnet, William Appleman, Herbert Marcuse, and Charles Taylor.[19]

Appropriately, the group now called themselves the "People's Christian Coalition." Their movement caught the attention of the seminary's donors, some of whom withheld contributions, and even the FBI who investigated them.[20] Throughout the early 1970s the coalition formed a loosely knit

---

18 Ibid., 71.

19 Dennis MacDonald, "Prophetic Resistance," *Sojourners*, March 1, 1972, https://sojo.net/magazine/spring-1972/prophetic-resistance; Dennis MacDonald, "Demythologizing the Present," *Sojourners*, March 1, 1973, https://sojo.net/magazine/march-april-1973/demythologizing-present; Joe Mulligan, "Thomas Merton's Secular Journal," *Sojourners*, March 1, 1973, https://sojo.net/magazine/march-april-1973/thomas-mertons-secular-journal; Boyd Reese, "America's Empire," *Sojourners*, November 1, 1973, https://sojo.net/magazine/november-december-1973/americas-empire; Boyd Reese, "The Structure of Power," *Sojourners*, January 1, 1974, https://sojo.net/magazine/january-1974/structure-power; Adam Finnerty, "The Christian Model," *Sojourners*, May 1, 1974, https://sojo.net/magazine/may-1974/christian-model; Walter Wink, "Unmasking the Powers," *Sojourners*, October 1, 1978, https://sojo.net/magazine/october-1978/unmasking-powers.

20 Wallis, *The New Radical*, 78.

commune which moved throughout the Chicago area. Finally, in 1975 "18 adults, two babies, a dog, and a cat arrived in Washington, D.C." where they continued their publication under the new name, "Sojourners."[21]

In *Agenda for Biblical People*, Wallis explained the purpose of *Sojourners* by comparing it to the 1930s Catholic Worker movement. He described Dorothy Day, a Marxist convert to Catholicism and the founder of the movement, as "the most thoroughly evangelical Christian" for her "works of mercy," attack on "systems which lead to oppression and war," and "loyalty to the teachings and traditions of the church."[22] In Wallis' mind, the "same combination of conservative religion and radical politics" motivated both his and Day's organizations.[23]

Wallis also wanted his Christian faith, reborn and reshaped by New Left ideas, to transform the broader evangelical world. Encouragingly, conditions in evangelicalism were moving in a direction which appeared fertile for his brand of religion. In 1976, Wallis predicted that "more Christians" would "come to view the world through Marxist eyes" due to "young evangelicals" and their "zeal for social change."[24] This kind of impatience with the status quo, and desire to change society, were exemplified well in Jim Wallis' influential friend Wes Granberg-Michaelson.

21 Joyce Hollyday, "A Little History . . . " *Sojourners*, September 1, 1981, https://sojo.net/magazine/september-1981/little-history.
22 Dorothy Day, "Catholic Worker Movement," *The Catholic Worker*, May 1936, https://www.catholicworker.org/dorothyday/articles/300.html; Wallis, *The New Radical*, 158.
23 Wallis, *The New Radical*, 159.
24 Jim Wallis, "Liberation and Conformity," *Sojourners*, September 1, 1976, https://sojo.net/magazine/september-1976/liberation-and-conformity.

CHAPTER TWO

WES GRANBERG-MICHAELSON

WES GRANBERG-MICHAELSON ENJOYED AN UPBRINGING thoroughly saturated in mainstream evangelicalism. His family subscribed to Billy Graham's *Decision* magazine, his grandfather received the 1962 "Layman of the Year" award from the National Association of Evangelicals, and his family attended South Park Church in Chicago. Their "whole life was centered on the church."[1]

Granberg-Michaelson's interest in politics started in high school when he became "campaign manager for Carol Craigle, who was running for student council president." He, along with a young sophomore on the campaign named Hillary Rodham, wanted to "break" the "tradition" that females served as secretary while men served as president. This interest eventually landed him a position interning for Republican Senator Mark Hatfield and then advising Democratic nominee George McGovern's campaign in reaching evangelicals.[2]

Though he grew up in a strong conservative Republican household, Granberg-Michaelson's political views, along with his religious convictions, progressively changed during his college years. His Young Life leader, Bill Starr, steered him away from Wheaton College, an evangelical institution, and toward

---

1 Granberg-Michaelson, *Unexpected Destinations*, loc 134, 146, 320; Granberg-Michaelson's parents also served as "key lay leaders" under Bill Hybels after he graduated from college. Hybels later became a famous proponent of the church-growth movement. See loc 344.
2 Ibid., loc 528-530, 714, 725.

Hope College in Holland, Michigan, a Dutch Reformed institution. There he could kindle his growing interest in psychology and other fields by rubbing shoulders with "professors like Lars Granberg; Paul Jewett, a theologian from Fuller; [and] Dr. Bernard Ramm." Granberg-Michaelson wrote: "Hope College introduced me to the Reformed theological tradition that expanded my more narrow evangelical background, and convinced me of the need to connect my personal faith in Christ to the external realities of the world."[3]

After graduating from Hope, Granberg-Michaelson attended Princeton Seminary. The class "Models of Missionary Theology" exposed him to "revolutionary theorists from the Third World" like Regis Debray and Frantz Fanon. According to Granberg-Michaelson, the professor, Richard Shaull, "was teaching liberation theology before it had a name." In another course, "The Structure and Strategy of Communist and Revolutionary Movements," he read authors like George Kahin and became "convinced . . . that the [Vietnam] war was both a foreign policy disaster and a moral travesty." The professor, James Billington, became one of his friends and mentors. Granberg-Michaelson's new influences contradicted the values of his upbringing.

It was during this time that he rejected "the conservative, nationalistic political ideology that had seemed wedded to the evangelical world." He lamented, at the time, that it was his "great misfortune to have matured in middle-class, conservative suburbia" and received "religious training in a church which belong[ed] to the National Association of Evangelicals."[4] His chance to set a new course and put his education into action came in the fall of 1968 when he moved to Washington, D.C., to intern for the progressive Republican Mark Hatfield.

After Granberg-Michaelson's move, he received the first issue of the *Post-American,* which he gave to Senator Hatfield, who also enjoyed its contents.

---

3 Ibid., loc 499, 552-557, 562-564, 640-641.
4 Ibid., loc 666-672, 672-675, 678-679; Granberg-Michaelson summarized Shaull's belief that "the message of the gospel translated into a revolutionary paradigm for societies that were holding people in economic, political, and social oppression." See loc 675.

During Christmas break in 1971, he met Jim Wallis and the two became friends. This opened the way for Sojourners to come to Washington, D.C., Granberg-Michaelson to join the community, and Jim Wallis to collaborate with Hatfield. The political topic uniting them more than any other was opposition to the war in Vietnam. Granberg-Michaelson even secretly met with a delegation from North Vietnam on Hatfield's behalf in an attempt to persuade them to release POWs, a potential development which could have helped Hatfield politically while possibly hurting President Nixon.[5]

While Granberg-Michaelson did not have the same disillusionment with Christianity that Jim Wallis had experienced, his faith did change. He started attending Church of the Saviour which he believed was his "first experience with a church deeply committed to living out the whole gospel." The pastor, Gordon Cosby, believed in "addressing unjust structures and social needs with the vision of God's kingdom." In the Sojourners Community, he "first began to grasp the deep connection between the sacraments—communion and baptism—and life in the Christian community." He also cultivated a deep relationship with "Father Stephen, the guest master at Holy Cross Monastery," which became one of Granberg-Michaelson's regular destinations. He was particularly influenced by "the writings of William of St. Thierry, a twelfth-century monk and mystic." Eventually, he joined the ecumenical movement and worked first for the World Council of Churches and then for the Reformed Church of America. Wes Granberg-Michaelson had strayed far from his conservative evangelical roots. In 2007, his old friend Hillary Rodham Clinton reminiscently wrote to him: "'It's a long way from Park Ridge.' It has been for both of us."[6]

---

5 Ibid., loc 917-918, 427-429; Gordon Cosby also deeply affected Jim Wallis. See loc 46.
6 Ibid., loc 754, 759, 427-429, 1031, 1288, 537, 890-899.

CHAPTER THREE

SHARON GALLAGHER

WHILE JIM WALLIS AND WES Granberg-Michaelson made their way into the halls of national power, the "Jesus People" movement sought to establish alternative Christian communities in hippie enclaves. One commune called the Christian World Liberation Front (CWLF) emerged in Berkeley, California. The founder, Jack Sparks, started a newspaper named *Right On* in 1969 and hired Sharon Gallagher to write for him in 1970 until she herself became the editor in 1973.[1]

Gallagher grew up twenty minutes outside of Hollywood in the San Fernando Valley where she experienced a middle-class lifestyle and attended a church with "strict rules of silence" for women.[2] After a brief stint in modeling at seventeen, she realized she was "becoming more and more of an 'object,'" reflecting the values of the "cultural wasteland of L.A." At Westmont College, an evangelical school, she lived under "standards" which "were more middle-class American than Christian," including the fact that "a woman's status was acquired through the men she dated" and that at "the institutional level women were discriminated against" with more restrictive curfews.[3]

After moving to the San Francisco Bay area to work for *Right On*, Gallagher was asked to "write something on 'woman's lib.'" For the assignment she

---

1 Virginia Hearn, ed., *Our Struggle to Serve: The Stories of 15 Evangelical Women* (Waco, Tex: Word Books, 1979), 17.
2 Ibid., 93.
3 Ibid., 94

started reading "women's literature, beginning with *The Feminine Mystique* by Betty Friedan," a feminist highly influenced by Marxism and existentialism.[4] Gallagher resonated with Friedan's insight. She stated, "I found a name for the anger, rebellion, and loss of sense of self I had felt in college." She then began finding "allies" among "women who had become Christians out of New Left backgrounds, where they had been 'liberated' in some sense and saw no reason to give up their personhood on becoming Christians."[5]

Drawing from books like Georgia Harkness' *Women in Church and Society*, Gallagher was able to find "alternative ways to read certain controversial [biblical] passages." Similar to Jim Wallis' "fresh eyes," Gallagher "reread the Bible" discovering "whole passages" she "had never heard theologized upon by male theologians."[6] She concluded that everyone was "conditioned by a sexist society" and the solution was a "liberating . . . gospel message" which could overturn "traditional male interpretations of the Christian view of women."[7]

This liberation also addressed other systemic injustices. In one article, Gallagher articulated "the Christian hope" as lying "in the fact that, when Jesus died on the cross, God was repudiating all His power in order to lift up the weak and oppressed as an example of what His followers are to do with their power."[8] Whether the topic was Vietnam, global poverty, or racism, *Right On* addressed the issues of the day by finding answers in the Bible, even if they weren't the standard "Sunday School" answers.[9] "We're trying not to let major lies in our culture go unchallenged," Gallagher stated, "whether they come from Sun Myung Moon, Werner Erhard, or the Military–industrial complex."[10]

---

4 Ibid., 95; Daniel Horowitz, *Betty Friedan and the Making of The Feminine Mystique: The American Left, the Cold War, and Modern Feminism* (University of Massachusetts Press, 2000), 97, 201.

5 Hearn, *Our Struggle to Serve*, 95-96.

6 Ibid.

7 Ibid., 97-98.

8 Sharon Gallagher, "Woman vs. Politics in Mexico City," *Right On*, September 1975.

9 Sharon Gallagher, "From Right On! To Radix: A Short History," *Radix*, August 1979.

10 Sharon Gallagher "11-10-78 Sharon Gallagher," Westmont College, November 10, 1978, In *Chapel Podcast*, MP3 audio, 23:37. http://archive.org/details/podcast_chapel-1978-1979_11-10-78-sharon-gallagher_1000111066198.

Gallagher's convictions put her in an awkward position. She desired to abandon the evangelical establishment and even worked alongside "secular women's groups." Yet, she still wanted to hold on to her Christianity.[11] Instead of abandoning her faith like Jim Wallis had done for a short period, or rejecting evangelicalism as Wes Granberg-Michaelson eventually did, Sharon Gallagher strove to demonstrate the best version of evangelicalism she could.

After graduating from Westmont and spending a "little bit of time at Labri," Francis Schaeffer's retreat in Switzerland, Gallagher realized what a Christian community could potentially look like, even as her faith in mainstream evangelicalism diminished.[12] When she first came to the Christian World Liberation Front (CWLF), she was "attracted" by their "sense of the gospel's immediacy: they not only preached, they fed and clothed people." They were also "sympathetic to the goals" of "the political left" but rejected their ultimate solutions.[13]

The CWLF saw a weakness in secular approaches to social justice. For example, though they supported the efforts of the "War Crimes Committee" for their "effort to slow down the U.S. war machine," they also understood that unless man was distinct from the animal kingdom, no moral authority existed by which to condemn anyone for the crime of mistreating human beings, an understanding gleaned from Frances Schaeffer's explanation of the *imago dei*.[14] This meant they were able to keep their New Left ideas while sustaining them on a Christian foundation.

---

11 Ibid., 98-99.
12 Gallagher, "11-10-78 Sharon Gallagher," 00:56; Gallagher recounts her disappointment at a 1972 evangelism conference in Dallas. She noticed "one evening when international flags were paraded across the stage representing different countries of people who were at the conference and the only flag that got a standing ovation was that of South Vietnam." This prompted her to ask, "what was the nature of the religion being offered?" Gallagher told an audience in 1979 that "people were really concerned that we napalm babies in Vietnam as all Christians should have been. And we weren't taking them seriously" adding, "I don't see how we could have expected them to take our message seriously." See 9:02, 9:23, 23:07.
13 Gallagher, "From Right On! To Radix: A Short History."
14 The Editors, "The War Crimes Committee," *Right On*, May 1, 1971.

Gallagher expressed the mission of the CWLF as critiquing "the old world system" by "telling people what they're being called from" while also describing "in some ways the shape of the kingdom or the new world that we're calling people to."[15] This "new world," somewhere between the political left and evangelicalism, appealed to many young Christians who wanted to achieve New Left conceptions of equality, peace, and justice in the name of Christianity. Almost every leader in the progressive evangelical movement shared similar experiences to those of Wallis, Granberg-Michaelson, and Gallagher.

15 Gallagher, "11-10-78 Sharon Gallagher," 18:40

CHAPTER FOUR

JOHN ALEXANDER

JOHN ALEXANDER, THE SON OF a Fundamentalist pastor, became an evangelical civil rights advocate after noticing what he saw as a weakness in his faith tradition. While attending Trinity College in Chicago, Alexander discovered the school's dispassion for poverty alleviation.[1] He also became "distraught by the way evangelicals generally opposed the civil rights movement."[2] This realization catapulted him into a "decades-long process" which "was so confusing" he "questioned most everything" including "the existence of God, orthodox theology, [and] whether a decent person could be evangelical."[3] However, Alexander was able to rebuild a version of Christianity based upon "love" for "the God of the Bible" who cared about social justice.[4] He "grew a new appreciation for Bultmann and liberation theology" and "moved in and out of abandoning orthodoxy." His philosophy became, "it doesn't matter much what you believe as long as you care about peace and justice." Later Alexander admitted, "I may have been a socialist when I was young."[5]

After graduation, John and his wife worked with his parents at a black fundamentalist college in inner city Cleveland. This experience "awakened" them "to broad conceptions of social concern," causing them to focus on issues pertaining to civil rights. The family joined the NAACP, renounced voting for states'

---

1 Swartz, *Moral Minority*, 28.
2 John Alexander, *Being Church: Reflections on How to Live as the People of God* (Wipf and Stock Publishers, 2012), 83.
3 Ibid., 84.
4 Fred Alexander, "White Pastor, Black Church," *Freedom Now*, December 1969.
5 Alexander, *Being Church*, 84-85, 184.

rights and Goldwater, and started publishing *Freedom Now* in 1965, "a twelve-page newsletter designed to convince fundamentalist evangelicals to support blacks' civil rights and equal opportunities as part of their Christian discipleship."[6]

The following year, John began teaching at Wheaton college where students followed him, "especially members of progressive clubs such as the Social Action Forum, Americans for Democratic Action, the Young Democrats, and the Jonathan Blanchard Association."[7] Though *Freedom Now* failed to make inroads with "fundamentalist white Baptist Christians," a "new generation of radical young evangelicals" resonated with John Alexander's message.[8]

Alexander expanded the focus of the magazine to include another issue he thought evangelicals were in the wrong about. He started devoting time and space to opposing the Vietnam War. The magazine also took on "capitalism" which it stated created and sustained "much of the hunger, underdevelopment, unemployment, and other social ills in the world" while promoting "individualism, competition, and profit-making with little or no regard for social costs." Because it put "profits and private gain before social services and human needs" it was "an unjust system which should be replaced."[9] Alexander later expressed that he believed that many of his Christian contemporaries whom he thought were indifferent to racism, violence, and poverty "would have sat back in the 1930s and let the Nazis come to power (and some would have joined them)."[10]

John Alexander moved the magazine to Philadelphia in 1970, where he continued his critique of mainstream evangelicalism. *The Other Side* became the magazine's new title. While Jim Wallis, Wes Granberg-Michaelson, Sharon Gallagher, and John Alexander confronted mainstream evangelicalism forcefully and directly, others, like Richard Mouw, took a more diplomatic approach.

---

6 Swartz, *Moral Minority*, 28-29; Gasaway, *Progressive Evangelicals and the Pursuit of Social Justice*, 26.

7 Swartz, *Moral Minority*, 31.

8 Dee Dee Risher, "A Clarion of Justice," *Sojourners*, January 1, 2005, https://sojo.net/magazine/january-2005/clarion-justice.

9 Eugene Toland, Thomas Fenton, and McCulloch Lawrence, "World Justice and Peace: A Radical Analysis for American Christians," *The Other Side*, 1976.

10 Alexander, *Being Church*, 83.

CHAPTER FIVE

RICHARD MOUW

LIKE MANY OF HIS CONTEMPORARY young evangelicals, Richard Mouw experienced a crisis of faith prompted by the civil rights movement and Vietnam. Ultimately, Mouw left Fundamentalism over its "anti-intellectual" behavior, disinterest in "social justice," and "separatistic spirit."[1] Though his mother was Dutch Reformed, Mouw's father was more Fundamentalist, and so were many of his early influences. He bristled against the legalistic rules inherit to the tradition throughout his young adulthood and while a student at the evangelical Houghton College.[2]

As Mouw transitioned to secular graduate schools at the University of Alberta and then the University of Chicago, he was exposed to New Left ideas. Days before starting this new chapter in his life, Mouw was profoundly impacted watching Martin Luther King's "I have a Dream" speech on television. He realized that even evangelicals he respected were "often dismissive of, and in some cases even hostile to, the civil rights movement." Mouw was equally disappointed in their reaction to Vietnam, an issue he "found secular sources to be more helpful" in morally navigating, "than evangelical ones."[3] In his new secular environment Mouw rubbed shoulders with "Wittgensteinian defenders," "Trotskyites and non-Marxist socialists,"

---

1 Krista Tippett, *Khaled Abou El Fadl, Richard Mouw, and Yossi Klein Halevi — The Power of Fundamentalism*, April 18, 2002. https://onbeing.org/programs/khaled-abou-el-fadl-richard-j-mouw-and-yossi-klein-halevi-the-power-of-fundamentalism.
2 Swartz, *Moral Minority*, 136-137.
3 Richard Mouw, *The Smell of Sawdust: What Evangelicals Can Learn from Their Fundamentalist Heritage* (Zondervan, 2000), 39-40.

and became an organizer in Students for a Democratic Society where he participated in political protests.[4]

During this time, he "drifted away" and spent "a few years trying not to be an evangelical." Instead, he "explored alternative worldviews," "enrolled in advanced courses in social thought and ethics," and attended "ecumenical chapel services, Catholic masses, [and] liberal Protestant congregations." However, Mouw confessed the New Left and social gospel did not, in fact, satisfy "the deep places of [his] soul." He needed a place to "ground" his new "moral convictions."[5]

It was then he "discovered [Abraham] Kuyper's social thought" which helped him integrate his political activism with his Christian faith.[6] Mouw also reached back into his religious memories and imagined a "radicalism" toward social evil even in traditional hymns.[7] For example, he expanded the meaning of *I Surrender All* to include "'corporate' concerns" such as "our racism, our fondness for military solutions, and our ethnocentrism."[8] Mouw returned to evangelicalism while altering his version of it as he discovered more "nuanced" and "complex" understandings of Christ's love, God's providence, and biblical interpretation.[9]

Richard Mouw's example, through his writings, such as *Political Evangelism* in 1973, and academic influence, first at Calvin College and then at Fuller Theological Seminary, helped light the way for other evangelicals attracted to New Left ideas. His became the respected academic voice against the status quo while another young evangelical, Ron Sider, became the pastoral voice.

---

4 Richard Mouw, "Weaving a Coherent Pattern of Discipleship," *Christian Century*, 1975; Swartz, *Moral Minority*, 138.
5 Mouw, *The Smell of Sawdust*, 40.
6 Richard Mouw, *Uncommon Decency: Christian Civility in an Uncivil World* (InterVarsity Press, 2011), 161-162.
7 Krista Tippett, "Khaled Abou El Fadl, Richard J. Mouw, and Yossi Klein Halevi — The Power of Fundamentalism," April 18, 2002. https://onbeing.org/programs/khaled-abou-el-fadl-richard-j-mouw-and-yossi-klein-halevi-the-power-of-fundamentalism.
8 Mouw, *The Smell of Sawdust*, 41.
9 Krista Tippett, "The Power of Fundamentalism."

CHAPTER SIX
RON SIDER

FOR SOME ANABAPTISTS, LIKE RON Sider, many New Left ideas were not considered very new. Sider, who grew up as a Brethren in Christ pastor's son on a farm in Ontario, Canada, already took for granted "Anabaptist concern for peace and justice and for the poor." Sider also never imbibed what he called, the "God and Country stuff" common to Fundamentalists in the United States. His political activism started while a graduate student at Yale University. He lived in "inner-city New Haven . . . at the edge of and then in the center of the black community." After Martin Luther King, Jr.'s assassination and talks with his African American landlord's son, "an angry young man open enough to talk to a white person," Sider joined the NAACP and worked on a voter registration drive in 1967-1968.[1]

In 1968, Sider accepted a position teaching at "Messiah college's Philadelphia campus at Temple University in the heart of poor overwhelmingly African American North Philadelphia."[2] When Sider, and his wife, a "Mennonite farm girl" named Arbutus Lichti, arrived, they began to return to their "Mennonite lifestyle roots" and "started to buy . . . clothes in thrift stores" and drive "cars until they didn't work too well."[3] They also calculated what they needed to "live for a year" while permitting "reasonable comfort

---

1 Jo Renee Formicola and Hubert Morken, eds., *Religious Leaders and Faith-Based Politics: Ten Profiles* (Lanham, MD: Rowman & Littlefield Publishers, 2001), 159-160.
2 Ronald Sider, "Living with Rich Christians in an Age of Hunger," American Society of Missiology, 2019, video of lecture, 6:14, https://www.youtube.com/watch?v=g85cwDBqhj0.
3 Tim Stafford, "Ron Sider's Unsetting Crusade," *Christianity Today*, April 27, 1992; "Living with Rich Christians in an Age of Hunger."

but not all the luxuries."[4] The Siders adopted a "graduated tithe" which increased as a percentage as their income increased. Sider regularly taught a course which focused heavily on the problem of world hunger, and in 1972, he produced an article based on his teachings called "The Graduated Tithe" which was published in InterVarsity's *HIS magazine*.[5] Sider's tithing concept was central to his 1977 work, *Rich Christians in an Age of Hunger*.[6]

Interestingly, Sider later recounted that *Rich Christians* was a book he "had no business writing" since "biblical studies, economics, politics, [and] social ethics" were topics he "didn't know hardly anything about" when he wrote it.[7] Despite this, *Rich Christians* enjoyed a broad Christian appeal, being the first book InterVarsity Press co-published with Potter's House, a Catholic publisher, and selling "more than a quarter-million copies" by the early 1990s. *Christianity Today* listed it as one of the top 100 books of the century and *Eternity* magazine even put Sider on the cover of its April 1979 edition. Yet, not everyone applauded.[8]

Sider later recounted: "Carl Henry, the first editor of *Christianity Today*, called me a Marxist [and] Francis Schaeffer's sons considered *Rich Christians* to be one of the most dangerous books of the decade."[9] Accusations of Marxism followed Sider the rest of his career.[10] He tried to answer this objection in an interview with Derek Williams in the first edition of *Third Way* magazine in January 1977. Williams asked if "the Marxist view" was "different" than his own "position?" Sider responded that "one can learn something from the Marxist analysis although it's not right at many points." He believed "Marxists"

---

4 Ronald Sider, *Rich Christians in an Age of Hunger* (New York: Paulist Press, 1978), 175.
5 Sider, "Living with Rich Christians in an Age of Hunger," 6:14.
6 Fred Clark, "Rich Christians in an Age of Hunger," *Patheos* (blog), December 21, 2005, https://www.patheos.com/blogs/slacktivist/2005/12/21/rich-christians-in-an-age-of-hunger.
7 Sider stated, "I never had a course in politics. I had one course in economics: Economics 101. I was at Yale Divinity School in the 1960s for goodness sakes with some of the most distinguished professors of Christian ethics in the world and I never took a course in social ethics." See Sider, "Living with Rich Christians in an Age of Hunger," 3:45.
8 Ibid., 8:20; Stafford; "Books of the Century," *Christianity Today*, April 24, 2000.
9 Sider, "Living with Rich Christians in an Age of Hunger," 9:50
10 David Chilton's 1982 *Productive Christians in an Age of Guilt Manipulators: A Biblical Response to Ronald J. Sider* was the most prominent and thorough critique of Ron Sider's book. Lloyd Billingsley also critiqued Sider in his 1985 *The Generation that Knew Not Josef: A Critique of Marxism and the Religious Left*.

were "naive when they suppose that the human problem is solely due to social structures" since in reality "it's deeper than that," being "rooted in the egocentric character of human nature since the fall."[11]

For Sider, and other members of the evangelical left, Marxism did not go as far toward social change as their version of Christianity did. Richard Mouw recounted a time in the 1970s when he and Ron Sider "spoke to an evangelical audience about 'the gospel and the poor.'" One listener publicly accused "Sider's views about programs for serving the poor" as "not from the Bible" but instead, "straight out of Karl Marx." Mouw defended Sider by quoting the lyrics from a hymn used at Billy Graham crusades, "I'd rather have Jesus than silver or gold." He then quipped, "Once you've learned that kind of thing from George Beverly Shea . . . Karl Marx's economics can seem rather tame!"[12] This practice of reading concepts like structural injustice and collectivist solutions into general Christian teachings was a hallmark of progressive evangelicalism.

Like Mouw, Sider thought sin was "personal and structural." In a world he believed was "tragically divided between the haves and have-nots," it was important to fulfill the "divine demand for the regular, fundamental redistribution of the means for producing wealth." The church could even set an example by selecting a "Jubilee year" in which "all Christians worldwide would pool all their stocks, bonds, and income producing property and businesses and redistribute them equally." For Sider, passages such as 2 Corinthians 8:14 taught that God desired "economic equality."[13]

He believed God's economic will was held back by the "rich minority of the world" who devoured "an unfair share of the world's available food." This action was not victimless. "White" "affluent" Christians amassed "wealth while hundreds of millions of people hover[ed] on the edge of starvation!" The rich

---

11 Derek Williams, "The Weakness of Evangelical Ethics," *Third Way*, January 13, 1977, 3-4.
12 Richard Mouw, *Restless Faith: Holding Evangelical Beliefs in a World of Contested Labels* (Brazos Press, 2019), 81.
13 Williams, *The Weakness of Evangelical Ethics*, 4-5; Sider, *Rich Christians in an Age of Hunger*, 93, 223, 92, 87-88.

oppressed the poor. Even citizens of "affluent nations" were "trapped in sin" since they "profited from systemic injustice . . . an outrageous offense against God and neighbor."[14]

To compound the problem, the earth's resources were limited and nonrenewable. Sider proposed a global solution involving the United States and other wealthy countries increasing their foreign aid, directing the aid "through international channels especially the United Nations," and giving "food aid . . . only to the countries which are implementing" the UN's "land redistribution and population control programs." For Sider, the world was "a dangerously divided, global village" awaiting "a new model of economic sharing."[15]

Fortunately, Christianity possessed the answer to the dilemma. The "ethics of the Kingdom" as communicated in the Sermon on the Mount applied to the political realm. God was "on the side of the poor," and as Leviticus 25 suggested, "the right to private property" was "not as basic as the right of everyone to earn a just living." In one section of *Rich Christians*, provocatively subtitled "Is God a Marxist?," Sider recounted biblical passages that vilified the rich and exalted the poor. Christians should extend the command to love neighbor to "a billion hungry neighbors." Sider gave practical suggestions in *Rich Christians* on how to implement a graduated tithe, a simple lifestyle, and

---

14 Sider, *Rich Christians in an Age of Hunger*, 26, 76, 166; Sider's global emphasis accompanied a wider realization in evangelicalism that Western Christians had a responsibility for helping make the world a better place through meeting physical needs. Evangelicals started organizations such as *World Vision* (1950), *Compassion International* (1952), and *Samaritan's Purse* (1970). Neo-evangelicalism also harbored a utopian strain (despite premillennialism) which may have accompanied or reinforced the New Left's emphasis on global justice. Carl Henry lamented that because fundamentalists had "no world program" and were irrelevant "In the struggle for a world mind which will make global order and brotherhood a possibility." See Carl Henry, *The Uneasy Conscience of Modern Fundamentalism*, (Eerdmans Publishing Company, 2003), loc 169, Kindle; Mark Hatfield said, "we must offer the world a vision of its future built upon God's promised kingdom." See, Mark Hatfield, "Piety and Patriotism," *Sojourners*, May 1, 1973, https://sojo.net/magazine/may-june-1973/piety-and-patriotism; Peter Davids wrote in *Sojourners* that "redistribution goes beyond the confines of the individual community . . . across nations and continents." See Peter H. Davids, "The People of God and the Wealth of the People," *Sojourners*, June 1, 1975. https://sojo.net/magazine/june-july-1975/people-god-and-wealth-people.

15 Ibid., 148, 219, 216, 112.

communal living. The Bible offered a template for a "new community" with "structures to prevent great economic inequality."[16]

Despite his radical views, Ron Sider's calm disposition and affable personality earned him a position of respect in the budding evangelical left. He was able to bring together representatives from various parts of the evangelical spectrum for the purpose of accomplishing commonly shared political goals. Perhaps Sider's greatest contribution was organizing the meeting which led to the creation of the Chicago Declaration.

---

16 Williams, *The Weakness of Evangelical Ethics*, 5; Sider, *Rich Christians in an Age of Hunger*, 208, 72-77, 31, 175-188, 87-88.

CHAPTER SEVEN

THE CHICAGO DECLARATION

IN 1972, RON SIDER HELPED launch "Evangelicals for McGovern" and became the secretary for the organization.[1] A group of primarily "mainline Protestant denominations" had already organized a committee called "Religious Leaders for McGovern-Shriver," but John Alexander, evangelist Tom Skinner, sociologist David Moberg, professor Anthony Campolo from Eastern Baptist College, and other "suburban-league educators and editors" who cared about "social justice from a biblical perspective," wanted to pitch George McGovern's candidacy to a mailing of "8,000 evangelical leaders."[2]

For Richard Mouw, seeing "the words 'Evangelicals for McGovern' actually in print was an experience of sweet vindication." He recounted: "When we regathered after the evangelical diaspora of the '60s, we discovered that there had been a significant number of scattered, lonely and frustrated 'Evangelicals for Gene McCarthy.'"[3] Though the association did not even raise 6,000 dollars for McGovern, it did help "provide the basis" for two extremely important developments in the progressive evangelical

---

1 Brian Steensland and Philip Goff, *The New Evangelical Social Engagement* (OUP USA, 2014), 270; Barrie Doyle, "The Religious Campaign: Backing Their Man," *Christianity Today*, October 27, 1972.

2 Carl Henry, "Evangelical Renewal," *Christianity Today*, January 5, 1973; EFM chairman Walden Howard stated, "Evangelicals should be concerned about social justice from a biblical perspective. I just don't believe social justice is a high priority with Nixon." Ron Sider was concerned about Vietnam. "If Vietnamese boys mean as much to God as American boys, then a solution that kills Vietnamese instead of us is not a just solution." See Doyle, "The Religious Campaign: Backing Their Man."

3 Mouw, "Weaving a Coherent Pattern of Discipleship."

movement: the 1973 Chicago Declaration and the creation of Evangelicals for Social Action (ESA).[4]

Ron Sider coordinated the 1973 Thanksgiving Workshop on Evangelicals and Social Concern which produced the Chicago Declaration.[5] The Conference started "on Friday, November 23, 1973," with "about fifty persons assembled in the dingy surroundings of the YMCA Hotel on Chicago's South Wabash Street." Sider noted that "the life and sounds of the inner city punctuated lofty theorizing with sharp reminders of the harsh reality of racism and economic injustice."[6]

Sessions included speeches from a diverse array of participants. William Pannell, *The Other Side* contributor and author of *My Friend, The Enemy,* Foy Valentine, executive secretary of the Southern Baptist Christian Life Commission, Paul Rees, vice-president of World Vision, and John Howard Yoder, an Anabaptist and author of *The Politics of Jesus,* all spoke.[7] Ron Sider was the "chairman of an expanded committee, Evangelicals for Social Action," which planned how to build off the workshop's success.

Some elements were more extreme than others. Robert Webber, a theology professor from Wheaton remembered being "appalled" during the "economic responsibility" work group when a "successful businessman" asked if it was possible to "be rich and be a Christian?" After "each person responded … The consensus was that if he really wanted to follow after Jesus, he would need to give up his job, sell his belongings, and give the proceeds to the poor. Then he would be in a position to follow after Christ."[8] Webber thought this kind of puritanical thinking went too far.

Not every proposal was accepted in the final draft, but, after considerable disagreement, the group unanimously approved their crowning

---

4 Formicola and Morken, *Religious Leaders and Faith-Based Politics,* 160; Russell Moore, *The Kingdom of Christ: The New Evangelical Perspective* (Crossway, 2004).
5 Ronald Sider, *The Chicago Declaration* (Wipf and Stock Publishers, 2016), 11.
6 Ibid., 24-25.
7 Ibid., 43, 57, 78, 88.
8 Robert Webber, *Evangelicals on the Canterbury Trail,* (Church Publishing, Inc., 1985), loc 1220, Kindle.

achievement, the Chicago Declaration of Evangelical Social Concern on Sunday, November 25, 1973.[9] The Declaration itself acknowledged Christians' failure to demonstrate "the love of God to those suffering social abuses," notably the American church's complicity in a racist "economic system" and "institutional structures," the "imbalance and injustice of international trade and development," and the "prideful domination" of men over women. The document called for attacking "materialism . . . and the maldistribution of the nation's wealth and services," rethinking living standards, promoting "a more just acquisition and distribution of the world's resources," challenging "a national pathology of war and violence," and calling men and women to "mutual submission."[10] Reflecting on the statement, Sider stated the idea that "evangelism and social concern are inseparable and that individual and structural sin are equally abhorrent to Jahweh are among the more important theological affirmations of the *Chicago Declaration*."[11]

Signers included John Alexander, Sharon Gallagher, Richard Mouw, Wes Granberg-Michaelson, Jim Wallis, and many other up-and-coming leaders of the evangelical left. Carl Henry, a towering figure in mainstream evangelicalism, signed the statement but critiqued that while it "called for a bold attack on 'maldistribution of the nation's wealth and services'" it "remained silent about Marxism's inability to produce wealth."[12] Leading Fundamentalist leader Bob Jones, Jr. claimed the statement followed "the socialist-communist line" and was a "half-way house between Biblical orthodoxy and apostasy."[13]

Signers emphasized biblical motivation over any kind of affinity for Marxism. Foy Valentine declared, "As Christians we cannot believe with Marx

---

9 Sider, *The Chicago Declaration*, 28.
10 "Chicago Declaration of Evangelical Social Concern," Evangelicals for Social Action, November 2, 2012. https://www.evangelicalsforsocialaction.org/about-esa-2/history/chicago-declaration-evangelical-social-concern.
11 Sider, *The Chicago Declaration*, 30.
12 Carl Henry, *Confessions of a Theologian: An Autobiography* (Waco, Tex: Word Books, 1986), 348.
13 Formicola and Morken, *Religious Leaders and Faith-Based Politics*, 161.

that man is economically determined."[14] Ron Sider thought "Christians who abhor Marxist economic determinism and believe" in Christian supernaturalism should "follow the biblical call for identification with the poor and oppressed."[15] The main problem with Marxism was its godless materialistic foundation, not necessarily its ethical prescriptions.

One signer, Samuel Escobar, clarified that he did not believe in "Marxism dressed with the rhetoric of liberation theology," but rather "New Testament Christianity that takes seriously again what it means to call Jesus and only Jesus—not Mammon—Lord."[16] He explained, however, that Marxists were similar to "the ancient biblical prophets" who "spoke boldly" against "pagan kings."[17] Escobar described "the paramount Chicago concern" as focusing "on the divine demand for social and political justice" which transcended any endorsement of "capitalism" or "socialism."[18] In Christianity, there existed a third way to navigate a divisive political debate.

In general, the emerging evangelical left relegated their criticism of Marxism to its deficient materialistic assumptions and irrelevance in the face of a more biblical critique. Its conception of social conflict along economic lines, emphasis on equality and common good over private ownership, and redistribution schemes were features not condemned, but rather championed by young progressives. Foy Valentine declared that the commitment of "Karl Marx . . . was to change the world." He then described how "Christians" were tasked with "world-changing" which included "economic systems," "the structures of society" and "the world."[19] What Marx was unable to accomplish, Christians could.

Despite this association with certain aspects of Marxism, most media coverage was positive. *The Christian Century* predicted the declaration "could well

---

14 Sider, *The Chicago Declaration*, 60.
15 Ibid., 12.
16 Ibid., 131.
17 Ibid., 121-122.
18 Ibid., 121.
19 Ibid., 70-71.

change the face of both religion and politics in America."[20] George Cornell, a columnist for the *Associated Press*, declared, "This new concern is more enduring than that of the liberals because it is more strongly grounded on biblical imperatives."[21] The *Chicago Sun-Times* printed that, "Some day American church historians may write that the most significant church-related event of 1973 took place last week at the YMCA Hotel on S. Wabash."[22] *Christianity Today* called the statement, "admirably forthright and timely" with a "basic thrust" that was "absolutely biblical." Though, the article also noted that it harbored a "sense of ingratitude."[23]

For these emerging evangelicals, a synthesis of New Left understandings, such as the concept of "power structures," fit "very closely with" biblical ideas like "principalities and powers."[24] Most had found, like Ron Sider's brother-in-law Donald Dayton, a resolution to the "struggle to reconcile the seemingly irreconcilable in his own experience: the Evangelical heritage in which he was reared and the values bequeathed him by the student movements of the 1960s."[25] With the formations of organizations and publications like, *Sojourners*, the Christian World Liberation Front, *The Other Side*, and Ron Sider's *Evangelicals for Social Action*, which nationally launched in 1978, a new brand of evangelicalism was on the horizon.

20 Majorie Hyer, "Evangelicals: Tackling the Gut Issues," *Christian Century*, December 19, 1973.
21 "Endorsements and Reviews," Wipf and Stock Publishers, accessed April 22, 2020, https://wipfandstock.com/the-chicago-declaration.html.
22 Roy Larson, "Historic Workshop: Evangelicals Do U-Turn, Take on Social Problems," *Chicago Sun-Times*, December 1, 1973.
23 "The Purpose of the Person," *Christianity Today*, December 21, 1973.
24 Boyd Reese, "The Structure of Power," *Sojourners*, January 1, 1974. https://sojo.net/magazine/january-1974/structure-power.
25 Donald Dayton, *Discovering an Evangelical Heritage* (Harper & Row, 1976), 1.

PART TWO

AN ALTERED ORTHODOXY: THE FORMATION OF A NEW LEFT CHRISTIANITY

WHILE THE EVANGELICAL LEFT MIRRORED many characteristics of their secular New Left counterpart, they also resembled their more traditional parents and grandparents. Evangelical progressives believed their turn to the left was consistent with, and based upon, core Christian convictions passed down to them. Jim Wallis declared, "The gospel message that had nurtured us as children was now turning us against the injustice and violence of our nation's leading institutions and was causing us to repudiate the church's conformity to a system that we believed to be biblically wrong."[1]

During his time at Trinity Evangelical Divinity School, Wallis and some fellow students embarked on "a study of every mention of the poor in the Bible." After coming across "several thousand verses on the subject," one student took "a pair of scissors to an old Bible, and proceeded to cut out every single reference to riches or the poor." Wallis used the hollow book as an example of how the "American Bible" was "full of holes!"[2] Like Wallis, other progressives determined to "take on the evangelical world," and the world itself, "with Jesus and the Bible."[3]

---

1 Wallis, *Revive Us Again*, 15-16.
2 Jim Wallis, *Faith Works: Lessons from the Life of an Activist Preacher* (Random House Publishing Group, 2000).
3 John Blake, "Progressive Preacher: As an Activist, Evangelical Christian, Jim Wallis Challenges Religious Right." *Atlanta Journal-Constitution*, May 21, 2005.

Oregon senator Mark Hatfield, who helped support and cultivate Jim Wallis in his early years, became an example of this thinking for younger evangelicals.[4] One critic complained, "One Sunday he will give us as liberal a speech as you will want and the next Sunday will come out with a fundamentalist talk."[5] In the March 1975 edition of *Right On*, published by the Christian World Liberation Front, two articles by Hatfield appeared. In one, the senator from Oregon chided the State and Agriculture Departments, along with "large corporate commercial agricultural enterprises," for their complicity in world hunger ,while, simultaneously, he encouraged readers to live up to biblical and historical examples of Christian charity. In the other article, Hatfield used Lent observance to promote twenty four ways Christians could fight world hunger. David Swartz notes that while "CWLF's politics were transformed, the foundations of their faith were not . . . Biblical allusions and spiritual disciplines coursed through their daily lives."[6]

Though young progressive Christians, especially those impacted by the "Jesus People" movement, often changed the expression of their faith by adopting casual language, music, and clothing in corporate worship, their modifications did have limits. They were careful to avoid the pitfall of mainline denominations by preserving a foundational belief in the authority of Scripture. Ron Sider characterized interest surrounding Evangelicals for McGovern as "a rising tide of theologically orthodox Christians who are not chained to conservative politics."[7] These "younger evangelicals," Sider observed, followed a "biblical faith" which "reaffirmed the centrality of

---

4 At Mark Hatfield's direction, Jim Wallis renamed his "Post-Americans" to "Sojourners" and moved to Washington D.C. where he wrote policy for the senator. See David Swartz, "The Evangelical Left and the Politicization of Evangelicalism," in *American Evangelicalism: George Marsden and the State of American Religious History*, (Notre Dame, Indiana: University of Notre Dame Press, 2014), 277.

5 Robert Eells and Bartell Nyberg, *Lonely Walk: The Life of Senator Mark Hatfield*, (Christian Herald Books, 1979), 16.

6 Swartz, *Moral Minority*, 96.

7 Ronald Sider, "An Evangelical Theology of Liberation," In *Perspectives on Evangelical Theology*, 117–34, (Baker, 1979), 128.

evangelism but at the same time insisted that social justice is also a central part of our biblical responsibility."[8]

It was this affinity for the Bible which set the progressive evangelical movement apart from the secular New Left. Author Craig Gay saw no "significant [ideological] differences" between "groups such as Sojourners" and "their secular counterparts" except for the fact that progressive evangelicals "attempted to justify" the same set of shared ideas "biblically."[9] As a result, the evangelical left developed a new vocabulary by synthesizing terms like "biblical," "gospel," "sin," and "church" with the New Left's language of social "power," "liberation," "oppression," and "equality."

---

8 Ronald, Sider, "History Shows Us Why Being Evangelical Matters." *Christianity Today*, November 26, 2016. https://www.christianitytoday.com/ct/2016/november-web-only/history-shows-us-why-being-evangelical-matters.html.

9 Gay, 55.

CHAPTER EIGHT

A BIBLICAL BASIS

CHRISTIAN FEMINISTS WERE ESPECIALLY VOCAL about their "biblical" position, and perhaps, more than any other quarter of the evangelical left, compelled to make hermeneutically sophisticated supporting arguments. Letha Scanzoni, who attended both Youth for Christ meetings and Moody Bible Institute became disillusioned with fundamentalism's approach to the role of women, but continued to embrace evangelicalism.[1] In a 1978 *Christianity Today* interview entitled "Evangelical Feminists," Scanzoni testified that she and others in her movement "did not become feminists and then try to fit ... Christianity into feminist ideology." Instead, she declared that Christian feminists "were convinced that the church had strayed from a correct understanding of God's will for women."[2]

Virginia Ramey Mollenkott, who earned her undergraduate degree at the fundamentalist Bob Jones University, promoted "biblical feminism," which she maintained was rooted "firmly in the major scriptural doctrines of the Trinity, of creation in the image of God, of the incarnation, and of regeneration." In order to "properly" understand the Bible's support for the "central tenets of feminism," Mollenkott emphasized passages challenging patriarchal assumptions of the cultures in which they were written. God's universal

---

1 Kendra Weddle and Jann Aldredge-Clanton, *Building Bridges: Letha Dawson Scanzoni and Friends*, (Wipf and Stock Publishers, 2018), 12-14, 59; Janene Putman, "An Interview with Letha Dawson Scanzoni," *Christian Feminism Today*, March 21, 2019, https://eewc.com/an-interview-with-letha-dawson-scanzoni.
2 Phyllis Alsdurf, "Evangelical Feminists: Ministry Is the Issue," *Christianity Today*, July 21, 1978.

plan for the role of women needed to be distinguished from biblical cultures which also upheld "slavery" and "monarchy."[3]

The Apostle Paul was "an honest man in conflict with himself" who struggled with "vestiges of" his "rabbinical training" in texts such as "1 Corinthians 14:34, where women are commanded to be under obedience." On the other hand, Mollenkott theorized that passages such as Galatians 3:28, where all are "one in Christ Jesus," showed the apostle knew "eventually the principles of the gospel would bring about a more egalitarian society." God's intention for mutual submission and spiritual equality, along with examples of women leaders in the Bible and maternal metaphors for God, constituted a defense of biblical feminism.[4]

In supporting her feminist readings of Scripture, Ron Sider's sister and Post American contributing editor, Lucille Sider Dayton, posited "four hermeneutical principles:" Taking "seriously those passages that suggest equality," paying "close attention to historical context," looking for "theological principles that are universal and eternal" instead of "time-bound and particular practical injunctions," and interpreting "the Bible in the light of [Christ's] words and actions," whom she described as "the great Liberator of all oppressed people."[5]

Daughters of Sarah, a popular Christian feminist magazine founded in 1974 by Dayton, described Christian feminism as "committed to Scripture" and "rooted in a historical tradition of women who have served God."[6] The same year, Letha Scanzoni and Nancy Hardesty, who earned her bachelor's degree from Wheaton and worked at Trinity College, argued for "egalitarian marriage" and women pastors in the extremely popular,

3 Virginia Ramey Mollenkott, "Women and the Bible," *Sojourners*, February 1, 1976. https://sojo.net/magazine/february-1976/women-and-bible.

4 Ibid.

5 Lucille Sider Dayton, "The Feminist Movement and Scripture." *Sojourners*, August 1, 1974. https://sojo.net/magazine/august-september-1974/feminist-movement-and-scripture.

6 David Swartz, "Re-Baptizing Evangelicalism," in *The Activist Impulse: Essays on the Intersection of Evangelicalism and Anabaptism*, ed. Jared Burkholder and David Cramer (Wipf and Stock Publishers, 2012), 285.

All We're Meant to Be: A Biblical Approach to Women's Liberation.[7] The "gospel," affirmed the authors, "would gradually undermine society's oppressive policies and restore God's intended harmony."[8] The evangelical feminist movement was gaining momentum and women were also not the only ones making such arguments.

In 1974, Jim Wallis claimed that a "distorted exegesis" was "used by men to support a status quo that subordinates women."[9] The next year, Paul Jewett, a Fuller Seminary theology professor, published *Man as Male and Female,* arguing for egalitarian gender roles based on the coequal fellowship of the Trinity and the separation in the Apostle Paul's writings between rabbinically influenced passages and inspired texts.[10] Wes Granberg-Michaelson became "involved in the national conference of the Evangelical Women's Caucus" in 1975, committed himself to "Christian feminism," and most importantly, explored "the understanding of several biblical passages on marriage as well as male-female roles and relationships." He and his wife Karin Granberg decided to change their last name to "Granberg-Michaelson" to reflect their belief in "mutual submission."[11] The same kind of logic used to promote feminism within evangelicalism was also sometimes used to support the normalization of homosexuality.

Normalizing homosexuality was not a main concern for the evangelical left originally.[12] However, there are a few notable examples of more progressive-minded evangelicals attempting to form what they saw as a

---

7 Letha Scanzoni, "The Life and Ministry of Nancy A. Hardesty," *Christian Feminism Today,* January 22, 2012. https://eewc.com/life-ministry-nancy-hardesty/; Letha Scanzoni and Nancy Hardesty, *All We're Meant to Be: A Biblical Approach to Women's Liberation* (Word Books, 1974. 84), 169-181.
8 Scanzoni and Hardesty, *All We're Meant to Be,* 72.
9 Cheryl Forbes, "Survey Results: Changing Church Roles for Women?," *Christianity Today,* September 27, 1974.
10 FitzGerald, *The Evangelicals,* 656-657.
11 Granberg-Michaelson, *Unexpected Destinations,* loc 1566-1568.
12 In 1978, Richard Quebedeaux stated that "Left evangelicals, except members of the Evangelical Women's Caucus, who regularly discuss lesbianism as a feminist issue, have generally dodged the question of homosexuality." See Richard Quebedeaux, *The Worldly Evangelicals* (Harper & Row, 1978), 129.

biblical correction to previous Christian belief on the topic. The Metropolitan Community Church, formed in 1968 by a Moody Bible Institute graduate named Troy Perry, had a statement of faith similar to the National Association of Evangelicals, yet a mission toward "meaningful social action" toward the "gay community itself." Richard Quebedeaux wrote that, "unlike some of his mainstream ecumenical liberal counterparts, Perry has made an honest attempt to find a biblical justification for homosexual life and practice." In a church pamphlet entitled, "Homosexuality: What the Bible Does . . . and Does Not Say!," the denomination affirmed that "in the New Testament, only homosexual activity motivated by lust is really condemned."[13]

As the 1970s progressed, some evangelicals started making a "distinction between homosexual orientation and practice." A few articles started to appear in "young evangelical publications like *The Wittenburg Door, Radix, The Other Side, and Sojourners*" which framed the issue in more compassionate terms.[14] Lewis Smedes, a professor at Fuller Theological Seminary, published *Sex for Christians* in 1976, in which he tried to "let the biblical message control [his] reasoning." Smedes argued that in the "tragic situation" of a homosexual who could "manage neither change nor celibacy," he could "develop permanent associations . . . in which respect and regard for the other as a person dominate their sexual relationship."[15] In other words, homosexual behavior was an acceptable last resort for a Christian with same-sex desire.

---

13 Ibid., 108; By 1978 the MCC had "over 90 congregations, 100 ordained clergy, and 20,000 members, mostly in urban centers where gays tend to live." See Quebedeaux, *The Worldly Evangelicals*, 129.

14 A concurrent broader softening on gender norms was taking place in the culture at large, including within evangelicalism. In 1972, Bruce Larson, a Princeton seminary graduate and Presbyterian minister wrote *Ask Me to Dance*, in which he stated, "There is no one who needs to be more enlightened about sex than those of us who have had a Christian upbringing." Larson believed that biblically unsubstantiated character traits were assigned to men and women which, in some cases, contributed to them thinking they may be homosexual simply because they failed to fit into culturally defined sexual categories. See Randall Balmer, *Encyclopedia of Evangelicalism* (Westminster John Knox Press, 2002), 331; Bruce Larson, *Ask Me to Dance* (Words Books, 1972), 91; Quebedeaux, *The Young Evangelicals*, 106.

15 Lewis Smedes, *Sex for Christians: The Limits and Liberties of Sexual Living* (Eerdmans, 1976), 12, 148.

Ralph Blair, a "former Inter-Varsity staffer," started Evangelicals Concerned the same year in order to deal "realistically with homosexuality in the evangelical community and about the implications of the Gospel in the lives of gay men and women."[16] Blair reasoned that it was in the best interest of the "early Hebrews" to oppose homosexuality because of a cultural context which called for higher levels of conception to continue the community.[17] Richard Quebedeaux noted, "gay evangelicals employ essentially the same hermeneutical approach as Paul K. Jewett. The Bible is culturally conditioned, and not everything therein is eternally authoritative."[18] In 1977, Blair participated in an ecumenical "Gay and Christian" conference which promoted the idea that "the homosexual condition is according to God's created plan."[19]

Because feminist and homosexual interpretations of the Bible were designed to overcome obstacles within the text, they were often rather complicated. However, most biblical arguments for social justice were simple. Their aim was to infuse New Left concepts into broadly conceived Christian moral categories like justice and love. The Bible was full of stories and teachings progressive evangelicals used to illustrate their preconceived understandings.

In 1973, Richard Mouw observed that evangelicals who desired "a more social and political witness" appealed "solely or mostly to the Old Testament prophets."[20] Their indictment of Israel paralleled the New Left critique of America. Passages from Isaiah, Jeremiah, and Amos were especially relied on to forward anti-war sentiment, equitable income redistribution, and the elimination of racial barriers.

One commonly cited passage was Amos 5:24, "But let justice roll down like waters And righteousness like an ever-flowing stream."[21] Clark Pinnock, Jim Wallis' mentor and a professor at Trinity Evangelical Divinity School,

---

16 Quebedeaux, *The Worldly Evangelicals*, 130.
17 Ralph Blair, *An Evangelical Look at Homosexuality* (Homosexual Community Counseling Center, 1972), 2-3.
18 Quebedeaux, *The Worldly Evangelicals*, 130.
19 Arthur Matthews, "Graham Scores at Notre Dame," *Christianity Today*, June 3, 1977.
20 Richard Mouw, *Political Evangelism* (Books on Demand, 1973), 14-15.
21 New American Standard Bible.

interpreted the verse to mean that "true religion would necessarily revolutionize the conditions of life into which it came."[22] Senator Mark Hatfield quoted it when calling for a day of national repentance over inaction against poverty, high levels of energy consumption, materialism, and the stockpiling of nuclear arms.[23] John Perkins, a popular evangelical civil rights leader, titled his 1976 personal memoir and best-selling social justice treatise, *Let Justice Role Down*.

In Perkins' mind, there were modern "Amoses crying out today against" the "present economy." There were also modern "Amaziahs," the name of the priest who opposed Amos, whom Perkins described as "white," or "black people who are propped up . . . to seek their own glory by 'getting over' into the system." It was Amaziah's job as, "high priest of the system," to accuse Amos of not being "a patriot but a communist and a heathen and a liberal—and not even a Christian."[24]

Progressive evangelicals' approach to the Old Testament mirrored interpretations given by civil rights leaders and liberation theologians. Because the Old Testament primarily focused on God's covenant relationship with Israel, categories of national sin, repentance, and judgment were present in its narrative and apocalyptic sections. Prophetic statements and biblical imagery indicting ancient cultures were then paralleled with critiques of current injustice in present systems. Members of the evangelical left often specifically applied New Left solutions while working from general biblical principles and commands.

Peter Davids, a writer for *Sojourners* and graduate of both Wheaton and Trinity Evangelical, believed the Old Testament portrayed a "denationalized people of God" who were members of a "political system which periodically

22 Swartz, *Moral Minority*, 54; Clark Pinnock, "The Christian Revolution," *Sojourners*, September 1, 1971. https://sojo.net/magazine/fall-1971/christian-revolution.
23 Mark Hatfield, "On Repentance and National Humiliation," *Sojourners*, April 1, 1974. https://sojo.net/magazine/april-1974/repentance-and-national-humiliation.
24 John Perkins, "Stoning the Prophets," *Sojourners*, (February 1, 1978). https://sojo.net/magazine/february-1978/stoning-prophets.

redistributes wealth." For Davids, Jesus' teaching represented an even "more thorough redistribution of wealth and a caring for the poor." Thus, Christians ought to obey the "command of their master" in participating in the "redistribution of wealth."[25]

Members of the religious left often took New Testament passages at face value, applying them to contemporary social situations. After becoming disillusioned with the "Marxist analysis" which had attracted him for years, Jim Wallis found in Matthew 25 what he believed "would transform both personal and political life."[26] In verse 45 Jesus states, "Truly I say to you, to the extent that you did not do it to one of the least of these, you did not do it to Me." Wallis reasoned, "How much we love Jesus . . . is determined by how much we serve those who are at the bottom of society." In Wallis' mind, his experiences in Detroit's Black community and in opposition to the Vietnam War were immediate applications of the text.[27]

Other New Testament passages on wealth were also easy to understand. Peter Davids interpreted Acts 2:44-47 as teaching that "God's people" should "give up their property whenever they see poor brothers and sisters in need." Likewise, the Apostle Paul's message in 2 Corinthians 8:13-15 paralleled: "From each according to his ability to each according to his need."[28] Certain sections of the Sermon on the Mount were favorite passages due to their emphasis on generosity and peace.[29]

Unlike Fundamentalists, who progressive evangelicals thought had voided the social implications of such passages, the new evangelical left strived for what they portrayed as a biblical understanding. The title of Jim Wallis' 1976 book, Agenda for Biblical People, testifies to this. They approached the Scripture with New Left assumptions and believed their reading was more accurate. The same could be said for the gospel itself.

25 Davids, "The People of God and the Wealth of the People."
26 Wallis, The New Radical, 69.
27 Ibid., 71.
28 Davids, "The People of God and the Wealth of the People."
29 Swartz, Moral Minority, 52, 115, 156.

Young evangelicals believed their parents held to a narrow spiritual and individual interpretation of the story of good news about Jesus' breaking the curse of sin and delivering His people. Instead, they also applied the gospel message to physical and corporate entities. A political understanding of systemic oppression, translated into corporate sin, extended the gospel's application. It was up to young evangelicals to recover what they thought to be the gospel's true and broadly defined meaning.

CHAPTER NINE

THE WHOLE GOSPEL

IN 1972, THE SOCIOLOGIST DAVID Moberg noticed evangelicals were "awakening to their inconsistencies and returning to the totality of the Christian gospel."[1] An expanded understanding of both the gospel and, as a result, the church's political obligations and corporate social responsibilities became a hallmark of the progressive evangelical movement as a whole. Expressing the Christian gospel included the "pursuit of real justice for all people" and "responsible and caring trusteeship of God's creation and its resources."[2]

John Alexander's father, Fred, stated, in the first edition of *Freedom Now*, that "to practice the whole gospel" meant "to have integration, to remove all forms of discrimination, to improve educational facilities, and to fight poverty."[3] Tom Skinner, a gang member from Harlem turned evangelist, frequently spoke alongside influential figures such as Billy Graham. At Intervarsity's Urbana conference in 1970, Skinner rejected the incomplete gospel of "liberals" and "fundamentalists." Instead, he promoted a third option by fusing both into an authentic gospel that would "free [mankind] from

---

1 Moberg expressed this total gospel as blending "evangelism and social concern." He states, ". . . old dichotomies between salvation and service, changing lives and changing society, proclamation and demonstration, man's vertical and horizontal relationships, personal piety and social service, faith and works, and believing and loving, all of which can be summed up in relationship to the contrast between evangelism and social concern, are breaking down." See David Moberg, *The Great Reversal: Reconciling Evangelism and Social Concern*, (Wipf & Stock Publishers, 2007), 212.

2 "A Response to the International Congress on World Evangelization," *Sojourners*, November 1, 1974. https://sojo.net/magazine/november-1974/response-international-congress-world-evangelization.

3 Fred Alexander, "Integration Now," *Freedom Now*, December 1965, 3.

the personal bondage of sin and grant him eternal life" while also addressing issues like "enslavement," "injustice," and "inequality."[4] John Perkins, a self described "fundamentalist" who Mark Hatfield called "a modern saint," shared the same view.[5]

While living in California, Perkins became burdened with the plight of young black prisoners whom he ministered to. This caused him to reevaluate his "real values and goals as a Christian."[6] Perkins moved back to his home state of Mississippi where civil rights workers approached him about the Voting Rights Drive. This led to his involvement in the movement. Later, Perkins recounted his sacrifice as he was "tortured in the Brandon [Mississippi] jail almost to the point of death" for his activism.[7] In 1964, he founded the Mississippi mission "Voice of Calvary," which included civil rights activities, such as voter registration, charitable endeavors like food and housing, as well as Bible classes.[8]

Because "evangelicals surrendered their leadership in the [civil rights] movement," Perkins believed they "had not gone on to preach the whole gospel."[9] In his thinking, "the purpose of the gospel" was "to burn through all racial, cultural, and economic barriers," "challenge all economic and social orders," call people to "fellowship," and make "a new family."[10] His goal was to break "the cycle of wealth and poverty."[11] The foundation for Perkins' ministry were "the three Rs: relocation, reconciliation, and redistribution."[12]

4 Tom Skinner, *How Black Is The Gospel: A Decisive And Truthful Message for Today's Revolution* (Skinner Leadership Institute, 1970), loc 709-715, Kindle; Tom Skinner, "The U.S. Racial Crisis and World Evangelism" (Speech delivered at Urbana Student Missions Conference, Urbana, Illinois, 1970). https://urbana.org/message/us-racial-crisis-and-world-evangelism.

5 John Perkins, "The Dividing Wall in America," *Sojourners*, February 1, 1976. https://sojo.net/magazine/february-1976/dividing-wall-america; Charles Marsh, *The Beloved Community: How Faith Shapes Social Justice from the Civil Rights Movement to Today* (Basic Books, 2008), 184.

6 John Perkins, *Let Justice Roll Down* (Baker Publishing Group, 2006), 75-76.

7 Bryan Loritts, *Letters to a Birmingham Jail* (Moody Publishers, 2014), 43, 45.

8 Marsh, *The Beloved Community*, 167.

9 John Perkins, *Let Justice Roll Down*, 99.

10 John Perkins, "Stoning the Prophets," *Sojourners*, February 1, 1978, https://sojo.net/magazine/february-1978/stoning-prophets.

11 Marsh, *The Beloved Community*, 182.

12 Loritts, 48.

Concerning the last "R" Perkins reasoned, "If the blood of injustice is economic, we as Christians must seek justice by coming up with means of redistributing goods and wealth to those in need."[13] Though Perkins disagreed with "liberal blacks like Jesse Jackson and [black liberation theologian] James Cone," he also thought they had "a great deal to teach" evangelicals.[14] Evangelical advocates for social justice, like Perkins, often infused what they considered to be biblical commands or results of the gospel into the message of the gospel itself.

Glen Melnik, an associate editor of *The Post-American*, exemplified this when he used the gospel as a call to obey ethical commands instead of as God's offer of salvation through Christ's sacrificial work. In 1971, he wrote, "The gospel says that it is wrong to kill for profit and power; that is what's going on in Vietnam. The gospel says that it is wrong to keep a human down because the person is a non-white in a white-ruled society."[15] Many progressive evangelicals, like Melnick, sounded similar to liberation theologians when they added New Left inspired social works to a term evangelicals had traditionally associated with grace to the exclusion of works of any kind.[16] In fact, liberation theology did influence portions of the

---

13 Ralph Beebe, "Voice of Calvary Has the Sound of a Friend," *Evangelical Friend*, November 1979, 4. https://digitalcommons.georgefox.edu/cgi/viewcontent.cgi?referer=https://www.bing.com/&httpsredir=1&article=1131&context=nwym_evangelical_friend.

14 Perkins, "Stoning the Prophets."

15 Glen Melnik, "Awake Thou That Sleepest or Who Are You Sleeping With?" *Sojourners*, September 1, 1971. https://sojo.net/magazine/fall-1971/awake-thou-sleepest-or-who-are-you-sleeping.

16 Latin American liberation theologian Gustavo Gutiérrez affirmed: "Although the denunciation of injustice has political overtones, it is first of all a fundamental demand of the Gospel . . ." See Gustavo Gutiérrez, *A Theology of Liberation: History, Politics, and Salvation* (Orbis Books, 1973), 118; Black liberation theologian James Cone used the term "gospel" in a similar way. He wrote, "Whites could claim a Christian identity without feeling the need to oppose slavery, segregation, and lynching as a contradiction of the gospel for America." See, James Cone, *The Cross and the Lynching Tree* (Orbis Books, 2011), 159. Jonathan Edwards, representing a more traditional American evangelical understanding wrote that, "the doctrine of justification by works" was "law" and "no gospel at all." Edwards asked, "What is the gospel, but only the glad tidings of a new way of acceptance with God unto life, a way wherein sinners may come to be free from the guilt of sin, and obtain a title to eternal life?" See Jonathan Edwards, *The Works of President Edwards*, v. 4 (New York: Leavitte, Trow & Co., 1844), 130.

evangelical left. Though it was especially associated with Marxist-inspired Catholics in South America during the 1960s and 1970s, its focus on social and political liberation as a fulfillment of the Christian gospel, appealed to some evangelicals.

Jim Wallis defined "liberation theology" as "a movement born out of the experience of oppression especially in Latin America" in which "the Marxist analysis and praxis" is "central." He believed liberation from "all the spiritual, structural, and ideological shackles which bind and oppress" was "the promise of God's salvation in history."[17] Wallis' mentor, Clark Pinnock, proposed an "evangelical theology of human liberation" which sought "to proclaim the biblical gospel in the context of a world of suffering, injustice, and inequality."[18] He thought it incumbent on evangelicals "to enter into the same struggle" as liberation theologians, by "hear[ing] the word of God . . . in a world of poverty and dire distress."[19] As Latin American and Black Liberation theologies gained popularity, so did their evangelical counterpart. Young evangelicals used the language of political and social liberation in many of their writings.

Wes Granberg-Michaelson thought "liberation theology" to be "most accurate and persuasive in its analysis" of "hope" for "the world's poor" resting "in liberation from structures of injustice." He floated what he called "pentecostal economics" based on the low value the church of Acts placed on material possessions. This was a way for the "American church" to avoid "capitalist captivity" while offering "the biblical hope of liberation."[20] Dale Brown, a professor at Bethany Theological Seminary, reviewed Jurgen Moltmann's *The*

---

17 Jim Wallis, "Liberation and Conformity," *Sojourners*, September 1, 1976, https://sojo. net/magazine/september-1976/liberation-and-conformity.

18 Clark Pinnock, "An Evangelical Theology of Human Liberation," Sojourners, February 1, 1976, https://sojo.net/magazine/february-1976/evangelical-theology-human-liberation.

19 Clark Pinnock, "A Call for Liberation of North American Christians," *Sojourners*, September 1, 1976, https://sojo.net/magazine/september-1976/call-liberation-north-american-christians.

20 Wes Granberg-Michaelson, "Liberating the Church," *Sojourners*, September 1, 1976, https://sojo.net/magazine/september-1976/liberating-church.

Crucified God for *Sojourners*. He concluded that it was a "masterpiece" for its extraction of "liberation theology from the motif of the cross."[21]

While liberation theology inspired many progressive evangelicals, most were cautious about adopting some of its characteristics. Clark Pinnock thought its appetite for violence overshadowed "the nonviolent servanthood of Jesus and the gospel."[22] Wes Granberg-Michaelson was concerned that while it could help evangelicals avoid "captivity by capitalism," it could also make them fall "into another form of ideological captivity by Marxism."[23] Wallis echoed this reservation stating, "the distinctive and decisive witness to the Word of God" could be easily lost in "conformity" to a Marxist system.[24] Samuel Escobar, a Perúvian Baptist and General Director of InterVarsity Christian Fellowship in Canada, expressed the progressive evangelical posture well.[25]

As a young man, Escobar rejoiced after Fidel Castro's triumphal entry into Havana. Yet, along with other Latin American evangelicals creating "a theology of their own," he had to evangelize and respond to secular Marxists on college campuses. This Marxist "pressure" helped forge a "contextual" understanding that "the apprehension of truth [was] to a very large extent a matter of perspective." A uniquely Latin American interpretation of Scripture, in which "the biblical text and historical situation" were "mutually engaged," motivated the rise of both Catholic liberation theology and Escobar's theology of liberation.[26]

At the 1974 World Congress on Evangelism, Escobar stated that "simple liberation from human masters is not the freedom of which the gospel speaks"

---

21 Dale Brown, "The Crucified God by Jurgen Moltmann," *Sojourners,* August 1, 1975, https://sojo.net/magazine/august-september-1975/crucified-god-jurgen-moltmann.
22 Clark Pinnock, "Fruits Worthy of Repentance," *Sojourners*, December 1, 1977, https://sojo.net/magazine/december-1977/fruits-worthy-repentance.
23 Wes Granberg-Michaelson, "Liberating the Church."
24 Wallis, "Liberation and Conformity."
25 "Samuel Escobar," Urbana Student Missions Conference, accessed April 30, 2020, https://urbana.org/bio/samuel-escobar.
26 Samuel Escobar, *Liberation Theology and the Development of Latin American Evangelical Theology* (Speech delivered at Wheaton College, Wheaton, Illinois, 2011), 6:25, 8, 19:40, 22:10. https://youtu.be/EP35aHIZvY0.

since "Freedom in Christian terms" meant "subjugation to Jesus Christ as Lord." Yet this "freedom" could not "be indifferent to the human longing for deliverance from economic, political, or social oppression." The "whole gospel" addressed the "poor, brokenhearted, captive, blind, and bruised" in their search for "freedom, justice, and fulfillment."[27]

In 1974, Escobar helped draft the Lausanne Covenant, which was signed by mainstream evangelical leaders like Billy Graham and John Stott.[28] One line in the document insinuated that "injustices" were, at least in part, caused by those "who live in affluent circumstances," who had a "duty to develop a simple life-style in order to contribute more generously to both relief and evangelism."[29] Escobar believed that "Marxism gave an answer to the problem of wealth and of property and means of production, but didn't give an adequate answer to the problem of power" since "once wealth is distributed, people do not automatically become good." This is where the Christian message, in which "Christ is there among the powerless," supplemented the Marxist critique.[30]

Dr. Thomas Finger, a professor at Northern Baptist Theological Seminary, demonstrated how Christians could "apply Marxist insights" from "Latin America's popular 'liberation theologies.'" Finger stated: "Marxism has much to offer: a set of 'scientific' tools for social analysis and projection of strategy. Here many liberation theologians distinguish . . . between Marxism as scientific analysis, with its own autonomy and objectivity, and as a metaphysical system. Christians may accept the first aspect (as a functional tool) while objecting to the second." Thus, Finger adopted the Marxist critique while

---

27 Samuel Escobar, "Evangelism and Man's Search for Freedom, Justice, and Fulfillment," in James Dixon Douglas, *Let the Earth Hear His Voice* (World Wide Publ., 1975), 322, 319.
28 John Stott, "The Lausanne Covenant: An Exposition and Commentary by John Stott (LOP 3)," Lausanne Movement, February 13, 1978, https://www.lausanne.org/content/lop/lop-3.
29 "The Lausanne Covenant," Lausanne Movement, August 1, 1974, https://www.lausanne.org/content/covenant/lausanne-covenant.
30 Jim Wallis, "Interview with Samuel Escobar," *Sojourners*, September 1, 1976, https://sojo.net/magazine/september-1976/interview-samuel-escobar.

objecting to it as an alternative to Christianity. Finger stated, "Insofar as capitalism is founded on selfish individualism and monetary motives, Marxist critiques can help flesh out, in economic and social terms, biblical indignation against these things." This was a "Marxist analysis, understood in the light of scripture and Christian praxis."[31]

Members of the evangelical left adopted a watered down theology of liberation which attempted to undergird Marxism with a biblical foundation by extending the gospel into the corporate world while still retaining a concept of personal redemption. The gospel was "good news" not just for individual souls, but also for the political and social systems that existed in modern states. Christ's death not only made a way for sinners to be in a right relationship with God, but it also paved the way for temporary physical liberation from unjust earthly structures. Some members of the evangelical left, like Richard Mouw, also arrived at this conclusion, but through a different channel.

Though Mouw was influenced by liberation theology, it was Abraham Kuyper's writings which helped him form a "political theology" for the church.[32] Mouw believed the gospel served as a lens for interpreting political needs.[33] Through expanding the gospel's function, he also extended the church's mission to identifying with the "sufferings of the world," and "seeking to alter the structures of the larger human community."[34] Still, Mouw capably navigated his way "between a privatized evangelicalism on the one hand and the liberal Protestant or Catholic approaches to public discipleship on the other hand."[35]

Mouw wrote *Political Evangelism* in 1973. His thesis was that "political action" was "an aspect of the evangelistic task of the church." For Mouw, a "full gospel . . . concerned with the whole man" meant that "Christ's atoning work

---

31 Thomas Finger, "Christians and Marxists," *Sojourners*, April 1, 1977, https://sojo.net/magazine/april-1977/christians-and-marxists.

32 Mouw, *Politics and the Biblical Drama*, 12.

33 Ibid., 13.

34 Ibid., 67-70.

35 Richard Mouw, *Abraham Kuyper: A Short and Personal Introduction* (Eerdmans Publishing Company, 2011), loc 34, Kindle.

offer[ed] liberation for people in their cultural endeavors" including "political institutions and the making of public policy."[36] This discovery fundamentally altered the evangelistic endeavor by recruiting Christians to "participate in the redemption and transformation of institutional life."[37] Proclaiming the Christian gospel included confronting "sinful structures."[38] In a 1974 article in the *Post-American*, Mouw explained:

> The payment that Jesus made through his shed blood was a larger payment than many fundamentalists have seemed to think. For even when they have sung the words with zeal, they have not seemed to acknowledge in their social/political lives that Jesus did, indeed, pay it all. He died to remove the stains of political corruption, and of all forms of human manipulation and exploitation. And he calls us to witness to and to enjoy the first fruits of that full redemption.

According to this concept of redemption, Christ's payment for sin could potentially extend to human structures in which the majority of participants may not even be Christians.

The motivation behind political evangelism was simply "the desire that political processes and policies preserve and promote the dignity of individuals."[39] This broadening of "Christ's atoning work" as a way to liberate individuals "in their cultural endeavors," including "the building of political institutions," fit well into the nineteenth century Dutch theologian Abraham Kuyper's theology of "common grace."

Kuyper, whose writings Mouw credited with helping him reconcile his political and religious beliefs, wrote about three kinds of grace from God: A particular grace, which applied to individual believers, a covenant grace, which applied to the community of saints, and a common grace, which

---

36 Richard Mouw, *Adventures in Evangelical Civility: A Lifelong Quest for Common Ground*, (Baker Publishing Group, 2016), Back Cover; Mouw, *Political Evangelism*, 14-15.
37 Mouw, *Political Evangelism*, 48.
38 Richard Mouw, *Politics and the Biblical Drama* (Eerdmans, 1976), 70.
39 Richard Mouw, "Political Evangelism," *Sojourners*, May 1, 1973, https://sojo.net/magazine/may-june-1973/political-evangelism.

applied to mankind as a whole.[40] He taught that God's common grace was responsible for things as varied as "prosperity . . . and health," Greco-Roman "philosophic light," "art and justice," "the love for classical studies," and "human virtue."[41] It reined in the curse of sin and served as the foundation for saving grace in unbelievers.[42] Kuyper even referred to common grace as a work of "redemption" displayed by the reality of life itself.[43]

Kuyper scholars Jordan Ballor and Stephen Grabill state, "Common grace, as Kuyper conceived it, was a theology of public responsibility and cultural engagement rooted in Christians' shared humanity with the rest of the world."[44] It provided a point of contact with the world whereby the Church could appreciate the "spark" of common grace within unbelievers and cooperate for the purpose of shared political goals that served the common good and furthered human flourishing. Kuyper maintained that common grace "cooperated with particular grace in amazing harmony, to direct God's work."[45] Richard Mouw later spoke of "common grace" as God's desire "to see cultural development move forward in the creation, even under sinful conditions."[46] He was not alone in his discovery.

Other members of the evangelical left were also able to reconcile progressive ideas with Christianity after exposure to Kuyperian "common grace." Wes Granburg-Michaelson "began at Hope College to absorb the Reformed voice" with its "emphasis on seeking an integrated 'world and life view.'" He wrote that "Biblical insights" were "in dialogue with the economy, politics, ecology, literature, science, philosophy, and the arts in the belief that in the end, all

40 Abraham Kuyper, *Common Grace: God's Gifts for a Fallen World*, Volume 1, *Abraham Kuyper Collected Works in Public Theology* (Faithlife Corporation, 2016), loc 635-657, Kindle.

41 Kuyper, *Common Grace: God's Gifts for a Fallen World*, loc 6029, 392; Abraham Kuyper, *Calvinism: Six Stone-Lectures* (Höveker & Wormser, 1899), 165.

42 Kuyper, *Common Grace: God's Gifts for a Fallen World*, loc 6187, 10907.

43 Ibid., loc 700.

44 Ibid., loc 191.

45 Ibid., loc 5857-5894, 10775; Brant Himes, *For a Better Worldliness: Abraham Kuyper, Dietrich Bonhoeffer, and Discipleship for the Common Good* (Wipf and Stock Publishers, 2018), 92.

46 Mouw, *Abraham Kuyper: A Short and Personal Introduction*, loc 590.

truth is one."[47] By graduation, Granburg-Michaelson's "thinking was shifting beyond the marriage of evangelicalism and conservative Republicanism" which had "deeply defined [his] family, church, and white suburban culture."[48]

Sharon Gallagher similarly believed her "intellect and faith could be integrated" and that the "gospel" had "implications" for "life" after following in the footsteps of the Christian apologist Francis Schaeffer, whom she heard speak at Westmont.[49] Schaeffer's thinking also had a profound effect on the CWLF. In an interview with *Right On*, Schaeffer's son, Frankie, expressed his father's theology well. He stated that a secular or religious divide within art did not exist. Instead, art existed "within a system of reality" and "the system of reality is what Christianity is, if it is absolutely true."[50]

Since nothing was spiritually neutral in this line of thinking even temporary political systems were redeemable and subject to the church's redemptive cultural mission. Common grace governed everything in existence. As a result, many progressive evangelicals believed they were recovering a complete version of the gospel. Not only was personal evangelism imperative for the amelioration of individual sin, but political action was necessary for challenging an expanded understanding of "social sin."

The editors at *Sojourners* classified any "attempt to drive a wedge between evangelism and social action" as "demonic."[51] Evangelism involved political causes. Using salvific terminology, Jim Wallis referred to "military and business leaders who" who had defected "to the peace movement" as "transformed from demons into saints overnight."[52] Virginia Mollenkott stated, "the

---

47 Granberg-Michaelson, *Unexpected Destinations*, loc 599-602.
48 Ibid., loc 660-663.
49 Gallagher, "11-10-78 Sharon Gallagher," 00:56, 7:18; It should be noted that Francis Schaeffer was very critical of Marxism calling it a "Christian heresy" and presenting Hegel's dialectic as its root philosophical problem. See Francis Schaeffer, *The Francis A. Schaeffer Trilogy: The Three Essential Books in One Volume* (Crossway Books, 1990), 44-45.
50 Dale Johnson, "A Conversation With Frankie Schaeffer," *Right On*, July 8, 1974.
51 "A Response to the International Congress on World Evangelization," *Sojourners*, November 1, 1974. https://sojo.net/magazine/november-1974/response-international-congress-world-evangelization.
52 Wallis, "Idols Closer to Home."

demon of sexism must be exorcised from the modern Christian community."[53] Interestingly, it seemed Christians were just as much in need of conversion to the "whole gospel" as non-Christians were. However, Anabaptist members of the evangelical left were not as likely to accept this line of reasoning.

Ron Sider disagreed with "the theology of liberation," as well as Richard Mouw's "broader definition of salvation."[54] He did not think there was "New Testament justification for talking about 'evangelizing' political structures," or that "salvation" referred to "social justice brought about through politics." For Sider, "redemption" was "not something that" happened "to secular economics and political structures" in the present.[55]

Yet, Sider also believed that practically speaking, "evangelism and social action" were "intricately interrelated" and that "evangelism often" led "to increased social justice and vice versa."[56] The reason for this was an understanding of salvation in which "coming to Jesus necessarily involv[ed] repentance of and conversion from the sin of involvement in structural evils such as economic injustice and institutional racism."[57] He believed that, "salvation for the rich" included "liberation from their injustice."[58] Though Sider did not technically apply salvation to social and economic structures, he still thought of them as inherently sinful and in need of destruction.[59] Thus, receiving the gospel required what Craig Gay called "a conversion to a particular kind of [economic] analysis."[60]

John Howard Yoder, an Ohio raised Mennonite, shared the same view. His theology professor at Goshen College, Harold Bender, taught that "first and fundamental in the Anabaptist vision was the conception of the essence of

---

53 Mollenkott, "Women and the Bible."
54 Ronald Sider, "Evangelism, Salvation and Social Justice: Definitions and Interrelationship," *International Review of Mission*, January 1, 1975, 254.
55 Ibid., 259, 261.
56 Ibid., 266.
57 Ibid., 265.
58 Ibid., 84.
59 Sider, *Rich Christians in an Age of Hunger*, 138.
60 Gay, 50.

Christianity as discipleship."[61] Bender believed that "discipleship" brought "the whole of life under the Lordship of Christ" which, in turn, allowed the church to criticize the "whole social and cultural order" and reject "what they found to be contrary to Christ."[62] Yoder accepted this understanding of discipleship and then became involved in a "Concern" group of graduate students committed to transform "North American Mennonitism" into a "more Anabaptist, more radical, more self-critical, less mainstream Evangelical, [and] less institution centered" movement.[63] To them, Bender had not gone far enough.

Yoder eventually taught at Goshen Biblical Seminary, and then Mennonite Biblical Seminary, during which time he published his 1972 book, *The Politics of Jesus.* In it, Yoder engaged in "an exercise of fundamental philosophical hermeneutics" by applying a "messianic ethic" in which the life of Jesus was the political norm.[64] In Yoder's analysis, the doctrines of justification and sanctification were not distinct, but rather merged in a broader concept of "discipleship, imitation, and participation." Yoder believed that the concept of "justification . . . by faith alone and through grace alone, apart from any correlation with works of any kind, undercut any radical ethical and social concern."[65]

Interestingly, Sharon Gallagher recounted how Yoder helped her navigate a "huge debate . . . between evangelism and discipleship people" at the 1974 World Congress on Evangelism, by telling her that there were not "two sticks to salvation." Instead, Yoder maintained, "We're not called to believe and then decide if we want to be disciples or not. We're called to be disciples."[66]

---

61 Harold Bender, "The Anabaptist Vision," *Church History* 13, no. 1 (1944): 14, www. jstor.org/stable/3161001.

62 Harold Bender, "Anabaptist Theology of Discipleship," *The Mennonite Quarterly Review* 24, no.1, (1950), 29.

63 Mark Nation, *John Howard Yoder: Mennonite Patience, Evangelical Witness, Catholic Convictions* (Wm. B. Eerdmans Publishing, 2006), 19-20.

64 John Howard Yoder, *The Politics of Jesus* (Eerdmans, 1972), x, 8-12.

65 Ibid., 212-213.

66 Gallagher, "11-10-78 Sharon Gallagher," 10:33, 11:12.

Progressive evangelicals, who appealed to liberation theology, sought to bring about a kind of salvation through the overthrow of what they thought were oppressive political structures. Kuyperian-influenced members of the evangelical left wanted to bring about societal transformation in part through redeeming political institutions. However, progressive Anabaptists made New Left prescriptions part of their personal discipleship and public witness. While Richard Mouw spoke of "taking responsibility for the structures" which were "created by God and affected by the redemptive process," John Howard Yoder talked about "witness to the structures."[67]

Mouw was thus able to introduce New Left prescriptions by eliminating the barrier between "secular" and "sacred," while Yoder achieved the same end by eliminating the barrier between justification and sanctification. For Mouw, the church existed within a framework, along with other institutions, of God's redemptive process. For Yoder, salvation and its social results were possible only within the boundaries of the church. Yet, their shared understanding of structural sin and liberation from it, whether confronted through discipleship or political evangelism, enabled progressive evangelicals, influenced by different theologies, to cooperate with one another in achieving the implementation of a "whole" gospel.

---

67 Tom Finger, "Reformed/Anabaptist Conversation: Jesus as Ethical Norm," *Sojourners*, December 1, 1976. https://sojo.net/magazine/december-1976/reformedanabaptist-conversation-jesus-ethical-norm.

CHAPTER TEN
A RADICAL COMMUNITY

WHILE CLAIMING TRUE BIBLICAL TEACHING and a more complete gospel, young evangelicals also tried to regain what they believed was an authentic understanding of the church. The "Jesus People" phenomenon, an organic movement built around Jesus' teachings and independent of the "organized church," increased in popularity from its local San Francisco origin during the 1967 "Summer of Love," to be featured in *Time* magazine's cover article in June of 1971. Figures like David Berg, a preacher's son and former Christian and Missionary Alliance pastor who left the pulpit after failing to move his congregation toward integration and sharing more with the poor, succeeded apart from institutional hierarchy.[1]

Berg's message resonated with alienated hippies. He endorsed "their rejection of American society, their parents' middle-class aspirations, and the thoroughly rotten 'system'" which included the "church," "educational," and "commercial" systems.[2] In 1968, at Huntington Beach's Light Club Coffeehouse, Berg delivered "Our Declaration of Revolution!" in which he castigated church traditions and structures such as buildings, denominations, Sunday services, pipe organ music, Bible colleges, preaching, education, alters, and ceremonies, in favor of revolution, communal living, truth, and loving God and neighbor.[3]

---

1 Larry Eskridge, *God's Forever Family: The Jesus People Movement in America* (OUP USA, 2013), 64.
2 Ibid., 65-66.
3 David Berg, "Our Declaration of Revolution," *The xFamily.org Publications Database*, September 1968. https://pubs.xfamily.org/text.php?t=1336.

In 1970, with around 120 followers, Berg started a commune on a Texas Ranch known as "the Family."[4]

Soon, disaffected hippies nation-wide formed communes such as Calvary Chapel's "Jesus Houses," "The JC Light and Power House," "Agape House," "the "Living Room," and "God's Forever Family."[5] While some, like the Christian World Liberation Front, did "mimic the speech and methods of the New Left," all were "inspired by both hippie utopianism and their interpretation of the New Testament" which "placed a high value on communal living."[6]

David Janzen, a member of "The Bridge," a commune in Newton, Kansas, wrote in *Sojourners* that "voluntary poverty" was a "clear emphases of Christ's message and life."[7] Ted Wise, who led "The Living Room," claimed the fundamental basis for the commune was a commitment "to live out the Book of Acts like a script."[8] In Missoula, Montana, an Evangelical Covenant Church started "Acts groups" which were "based on strong accountability and sharing," and "deeply influenced by the message of Sojourners." They "understood themselves as models for the renewal of the church."[9] Tom Skinner captured well the communal impulse when he asserted:

> What Jesus has in mind is, through a radicalized group of people, to produce a new community, a new order of things that will be a live model, on earth, of what is happening in heaven. So when the lonely and the despondent, the unloved, the despised, the hated stand up and say, 'Where has the love gone?' the new order, the

---

4 David Berg, "Revolution for Jesus," Accessed February 19, 2020. https://www.david-berg.org/mission/revolution-for-jesus; David Berg, "Creating a New Society," Accessed February 19, 2020, https://www.davidberg.org/mission/a-sample-community-deep-in-the-heart-of-texas.

5 Eskridge, 72, 76, 120, 29, 171; Eskridge states, ". . . by the summer of 1970, there were, at the very least, more than 100 Jesus People groups and centers functioning in Southern California." See Eskridge, *God's Forever Family*, 77.

6 Eskridge, 96, 55.

7 David Janzen, "The Empire of Mammon and the Joyous Fellowship," *Sojourners*, September 1, 1973. https://sojo.net/magazine/september-october-1973/empire-mammon-and-joyous-fellowship.

8 Ted Wise, "Jason Questions a Jesus Freak (An interview from Ted Wise)," Interview by Jason Cronn, September 13, 1997, https://www.pbc.org/messages/jason-questions-a-jesus-freak-an-interview.

9 Granberg-Michaelson, *Unexpected Destinations*, loc 1507-1509, 1753-1754.

new community, stands up and says, 'Over here! Love is practiced among us. We are the epitome of love, we live it out.'[10]

For disaffected youth hungering for belonging, alternative communities offered a family connectedness transcending partisan divides and striving for a pre-modern collective love. The Jesus People, in the words of one convert, "had something REAL" which did not match the hypocrisy found in traditional churches, but did match the "radical" Christianity exemplified by the early church and set forth in the pages of Scripture.[11] Even a "surprising number of 'pastor's kids,' as one member of "The Living Room" remembered, sought a spiritual lifestyle stripped of manmade traditions.[12] Jesus People rejected what they saw as their parent's hypocrisy, without rejecting their parent's Bible.

Even progressive evangelicals who did not consider communal living absolutely necessary, like Jim Wallis and Ron Sider, justified their anti-institutional lifestyles on the grounds "that Jesus came to found a community which would live in an alternative way to the generally accepted way of society."[13] Clark Pinnock postulated that Christianity had "revolutionary" societal implications and that "institutional" American Christianity had become a "counter-revolutionary force."[14] Instead, the true church represented a "new society," "sacrificial" toward "others," "genuine" in its "expression of God's love," and "prophetic" in "exposing and opposing of all demonic forces."[15] For some, a certain kind of public and political engagement became an unspoken statement of faith and test for fellowship.

Bill Lane, a *Sojourners* contributor, viewed his evangelical roots as a "spiritual home," yet felt like a "stranger" to his "own heritage" in the "arena of

---

10 Bill Milliken, *So Long Sweet Jesus: A Street Worker's Spiritual Odyssey*, (Prometheus Press, 1973), 12-13.
11 Eskridge, *God's Forever Family*, 279.
12 Ibid., 38.
13 Derek Tidball, "The New Gospel of Community," *Third Way*, April 1980.
14 Clark Pinnock, "The Christian Revolution," *Sojourners*, September 1, 1971. https://sojo.net/magazine/fall-1971/christian-revolution.
15 "A Response to the International Congress on World Evangelization."

Christian action" with respect to the physically needy "Jesus came to help."[16] In 1980, Ron Sider wrote in the *Christian Century*, "Those who neglect the needy are not really God's people at all—no matter how frequent their religious rituals or how orthodox their creeds and confessions."[17] Thus, ontologically, the church's existence hinged on its ability to correctly publicly and politically engage.

Progressive evangelicals, like secular New Left thinkers, opposed Western cultural hegemony. However, unlike their secular counterparts, they saw the church, not as a force of Western religious oppression, but rather as an organization outside of, and in opposition to, "worldly" societal habits and hierarchy. Jim Wallis maintained:

> The church must live in this tension and recognize the opposition between the world-system and the kingdom of God. The church is thus an inexhaustible revolutionary force in the world. Its mission is perpetual—not on behalf of nation, party, program or ideology, but rather on behalf of the kingdom of God, which may make it victim of the hostility of both the established order and of those who seek to overthrow it. Corporately, we must commit ourselves to build a church that is a sign of Christ's presence in the world and thus a counter-sign to the values of American society and power. The recovery of the church's true identity in the world is most basic to its political responsibility."[18]

Wallis' ecclesiology followed the same reasoning that Ron Sider, John Howard Yoder, Art Gish, and other members of the "disproportionate number of Anabaptists" in the evangelical left, promoted.[19]

Raised in Lancaster Pennsylvania, and a member of The Church of the Brethren, Art Gish was involved in the civil rights and peace movements as

---

16 Bill Lane, "New Directions for the Church," *Sojourners*, January 1, 1973. https://sojo.net/magazine/january-february-1973/new-directions-church.

17 Ronald Sider, "An Evangelical Theology of Liberation." *Christian Century*, March 19, 1980.

18 Jim Wallis, "Biblical Politics," *Sojourners*, April 1, 1974. https://sojo.net/magazine/april-1974/biblical-politics.

19 Swartz, *Moral Minority*, 153.

a young man.[20] Like other contributors to *Sojourners, The Other Side,* and the Chicago Declaration, Gish became aware of the "radical nature" of his religion after getting personally involved "with the New Left" and discovering "the radical heritage of the Christian faith in general and the Anabaptist tradition in particular."[21] Gish believed that the communal traditions of "Fransiscans, Waldensees, Unitas Fratrum, Collegiants, Anabaptists, and Quakers" had "found new expression."[22] While he rejected secular Marxism, he embraced what he quoted John Chrystostom as calling, a "communism of love."[23]

In his 1970 work, *The New Left and Christian Radicalism,* Gish postulated that in order to enact "social change" there would need to be "a synthesis of Anabaptist and New Left strategy" which broke "from the existing structures and beg[an] to create new alternatives outside the system."[24] Parallels existed between "social radicalism in the United States" and "Christian radicalism in sixteenth century Europe." Anabaptists had a "profound vision of a new society" which they lived in "as if it had already come," a "method of witness," through "creating separate communities," and a "hope in man's potential." For Gish, and other Anabaptists, "To be a Christian [was] to be a radical," an "extremist," and "in continual conflict with the structures of society."[25]

David Gill, a member of the Berkeley's CWLF, also justified his "radical" Christianity by appealing to the "left wing of the Reformation" comprised of "Anabaptist/Mennonite . . . heretics" such as "Peter Waldo, St. Francis, the Bohemian Brethren, the Quakers," and "John Howard Yoder." Gill explained that "being a radical Christian" meant "stripping off the centuries of cultural and institutional baggage," opposing the "individualism and unconcern

---

20 Ad Crable, "Arthur Gish, County Native, Global Activist Dies," *Lancaster Online,* August 9, 2010, https://web.archive.org/web/20100809235820/http://articles.lancasteronline.com/local/4/271775.

21 Art Gish, *The New Left and Christian Radicalism* (Eerdmans, 1970), 49.

22 Ibid., 17.

23 Art Gish, *Living in Christian Community* (Herald Press, 1979), 72.

24 Art Gish, *The New Left and Christian Radicalism* (Eerdmans, 1970), 123.

25 Dana Johnson, "The New Left and Christian Radicalism," *Review of Religious Research* 13, no. 2 (1972): 153–54, https://doi.org/10.2307/3509752.

nurtured by much of the established church," and taking Jesus' "critique of capitalism" seriously. For Gill, and many other Anabaptist-influenced members of the evangelical left, Christianity was about "discipleship (on the level of individual life) and the kingdom of God (on the community level)."[26]

Anabaptists believed that alternative living was a form of evangelism. John Howard Yoder thought of "the Church" as "a laboratory of social pluralism," "a nurturing ground for counter-cultural values," and "a lived alternative to a society structured around retributive sanctions." He stated that "the Church [was] both the paradigm and the instrument of the political presence of the gospel," and its "very existence" was "its primary task." It was the "social structure through which the Gospel work[ed] to change other structures."[27] In a similar way, Ron Sider emphasized the church's job to offer "a visible model of the way people can live in community in more living and just ways."[28] Dale Brown stated that when Christ "asserted that his kingdom was not of this world, he did not mean that it was entirely individual or invisible. Rather, he was affirming that the means were different."[29]

Anabaptists were not merely interested in saving souls for a heavenly kingdom. They also wanted to further an earthly kingdom through the lived example of alternative Christian communities. Their theological tradition justified the inclusion of New Left-inspired ways of living within Christianity. For progressive evangelicals, the true church, like the early church, necessarily existed on the periphery of culture, engaging it from the outside. Like the church, their version of Jesus was also of an outsider rebelling against an unjust status quo.

---

26 David Gill, "Toward a Radical Christian Identity," *Right On*, October 1974.
27 Sider, *The Chicago Declaration*, 102; Yoder, *The Politics of Jesus*, 150, 155.
28 Sider, "Evangelism, Salvation and Social Justice: Definitions and Interrelationship," 266.
29 Dale Brown, "Thy Kingdom Come," *Sojourners*, June 1, 1974, https://sojo.net/magazine/june-july-1974/thy-kingdom-come.

CHAPTER ELEVEN

AN UNFILTERED JESUS

FOR THE EVANGELICAL LEFT, REPLACING incorrect understandings of hermeneutics, soteriology, and ecclesiology were incomplete without also rescuing Jesus from what sociologist Robert Bellah called, America's "civil religion."[1] Historians have routinely thought of mainstream figures, like Billy Graham, as exemplifying a virtuous and nationalist conception of America, popularized by Lincoln, and laced with biblical imagery and a sense of chosenness.[2] Evangelical social justice advocates believed this template was diametrically opposed to the example of the biblical Jesus.

In 1971, Tom Loudon, an associate editor of *The Post-American*, opined in the first issue that if "Christ came back today," "militarists" would "call him a subversive," "nationalists" would "claim that he was not a true American," and "people would realize that he was a traitor" for calling them to live for "another kingdom." In short, everyone would think "he was trying to destroy the American way of life."[3]

A year earlier, InterVarsity Press published the sociology driven book, *Your God is Too White*, by Columbus Salley, a Trinity College instructor, and Ronald

1 Robert Bellah, "Civil Religion in America," *Journal of the American Academy of Arts and Sciences* 96, no. 1 Religion in America (Winter 1967).
2 Quebedeaux, *The Young Evangelicals*, 83; Steven Miller, *Billy Graham and the Rise of the Republican South. Politics and Culture in Modern America*, (University of Pennsylvania Press, Incorporated, 2011), 158; Michael Long, *Billy Graham and the Beloved Community: America's Evangelist and the Dream of Martin Luther King, Jr.* (Palgrave Macmillan US, 2016), 58.
3 Tom Loudon, "If Christ Came Back Today," *Sojourners*, September 1, 1971. https://sojo.net/magazine/fall-1971/if-christ-came-back-today.

Behm, the pastor at South Shore Bible Baptist Church.[4] *Christianity Today* promoted it as a work, "every Christian should read."[5] After declaring "the white Jesus is dead," Salley and Behm argued blacks "cannot identify or intimately associate with what they conceive to be a white, blue-eyed Jesus—a Jesus who negates the humanity of their blackness, a Jesus who demands that they whiten their souls in order to save them." Using the language of liberation theology, Salley taught "God must become black. He must become the God not of 'the sweet by and by,' but of the bitter here and now."[6]

Tom Skinner, in his 1970 book, *How Black is the Gospel*, also rejected the "Jesus from the white society" who was "the defender of the American system, president of the New York Stock Exchange, head of the Pentagon, chairman of the National Republican Committee—a flag-waving, patriotic American—and against everything else."[7] Ron Potter, a Wheaton student who helped bring Tom Skinner to speak at the Christian college in 1969 testified, "He helped us to differentiate between biblical Christianity and the Christ of the white evangelical culture."[8]

The image of Jesus conceived by progressive evangelicals was diametrically opposed to the commonly revered Jesus of the American consciousness. He was a counter-culture Christ who was not neutral on political issues and only to be used as a unifying social symbol for positivity and peace. In 1971, John Alexander published a sarcastic article in *The Other Side* entitled "Madison Avenue Jesus," in which he imagined American Christians giving advice to the biblical Jesus by telling him to be more well-mannered, gradualist, friendly with Pharisees, greedy, elitist, positive, patriotic, and image

---

4 Soong-Chan Rah, "In Whose Image: The Emergence, Development, and Challenge of African-American Evangelicalism," (PhD diss. Duke University, 2016), 199.
5 "Choice Evangelical Books of 1970," *Christianity Today*, February 26, 1971, https://www.christianitytoday.com/ct/1971/february-26/choice-evangelical-books-of-1970.html.
6 Columbus Salley and Ronald Behm, *Your God Is Too White*, (Inter-Varsity Press, 1970), 13, 73.
7 Skinner, *How Black is the Gospel*, 729-733.
8 Edward Gilbreath, "Thomas Skinner: A Prophet out of Harlem," *Christianity Today*, September 16, 1996.

conscious.[9] In the minds of the evangelical left, Jesus was not receiving a make-over from them. He had already received one, and they were wiping away the American makeup.

At the root, progressive evangelicals voiced much more than political disagreements with the broader evangelical world on issues such as welfare, integration, the Equal Right's Amendment, and Vietnam. They called the American church back to what they deemed a more biblical understanding of gender roles, social justice, communal living, and Christ's example. In the process, they altered how the Bible was interpreted, how the atonement was understood, how the church related to the broader culture, and how Christians imagined Jesus Himself. In the minds of progressive evangelicals, theirs was, in a sense, a conservative movement, away from man-made traditions and back to the basics of original authentic Christianity. When religious adherence and attendance fell precipitously during the 1960s, whatever cultural rebellion young evangelicals harbored, it drove them back to the faith of their youth.[10]

---

9 John Alexander, "Madison Avenue Jesus," *Sojourners*, September 1, 1971, https://sojo.net/magazine/fall-1971/madison-avenue-jesus.

10 Frank Newport, "In U.S., Four in 10 Report Attending Church in Last Week," Gallup, December 14, 2013, https://news.gallup.com/poll/166613/four-report-attending-church-last-week.aspx.

PART THREE

AN AMERICAN REVIVAL: THE RELIGIOUS ROOTS OF THE EVANGELICAL LEFT

HISTORIANS HAVE TYPICALLY IDENTIFIED THE First and Second Great Awakenings as the two major revival movements of American history. Both rekindled devotion within established churches while drawing new converts. Both resulted in social reforms and charitable endeavors. Both also contributed to the formation of a national identity. Progressive evangelicals thought they could possibly usher in yet a third awakening by purifying various Christian traditions, uniting them in a common social cause, and attracting young people influenced by the New Left. Theirs was a theologically diverse movement of socially like-minded believers.

As demonstrated, young evangelicals combined New Left ideology with a number of varied theologies. For example, Dee Dee Risher well described *The Other Side* as "ecumenical" and drawing "on the strengths of a number of traditions."

> From the Baptists and evangelicals, it took a seriousness for grappling with scripture and an emphasis on conversion. From the Anabaptists, it drew the importance of lifestyle as a vehicle for Christian witness and the conviction that peacemaking was at the core of Jesus' message. From mainline Protestants, it emphasized the social gospel, and from the Catholic tradition, it built on acts of mercy, attention to spirituality, and a sense of the liturgical

seasons in our lives. It was inspired by liberation theology movements and pentecostal movements alike.[1]

While foreign theological traditions helped justify the movement, the evangelical left still retained a character uniquely formed and existing within the stream of North American Christianity.

Though the emerging evangelical left disagreed with many of the assumptions of their parents and grandparents, the movement was not a clean break from either neo-evangelicalism nor fundamentalism. Not only did they meet standard academic understandings of evangelical belief and practice, such as the Bebbington quadrilateral, but many of their social instincts were uniquely evangelical as well.[2] This is not surprising since it was in the context of evangelicalism that young progressives spent their formative years.

In general, neo-evangelicalism enabled the kind of social engagement progressives participated in, while fundamentalism presaged the uncompromising militancy characterizing their engagement. If neo-evangelicals provided the basis, fundamentalists, and their nineteenth century revivalist forebears helped furnish the attitude. Thus, young progressives were not simply "taking over" American evangelicalism from the outside. They were "reviving" what they believed was a corrupted religion as insiders who owed much of their personality to American evangelicalism itself. Yet, politically the two movements were on opposite ends of the spectrum.

---

1 Risher, "A Clarion of Justice."
2 The Bebbington Quadrilateral is a popular tool which proposes four criteria by which to define evangelicalism: conversionism, activism, biblicism, and crucicentrism. See David Bebbington, *Evangelicalism in Modern Britain: A History from the 1730s to the 1980s* (Routledge, 2003), 2-3.

CHAPTER TWELVE

NEO-EVANGELICAL STEP CHILDREN

BILLY GRAHAM, CAMPUS CRUSADE FOR Christ, *Christianity Today,* and other mainstream evangelical outlets tended to reflect the political sentiments of their constituents. Conservative theology was associated with conservative political views.[1] Throughout the 1950s and 1960s, the National Association of Evangelicals (NAE) advocated anti-communism, the "rights of the private sector," and, similar to their fundamentalist predecessors, a "religious-friendly system of education," along with the regulation of alcohol, gambling, and obscene literature.[2]

This politically conservative default setting can best be understood as resulting from cultural factors apart from the influence of intellectual evangelicalism since evangelicals did not initially possess a secure politically driven ideological foundation. For example, the NAE did not specifically address policy implementation nor jurisdictional questions. They appealed to abstract, pragmatic, and secular arguments in trying to maintain a Christian-saturated American culture.[3]

Though they were morally certain, evangelical leaders did not develop positions on first order political questions and thus were not part of intellectual

---

1 Moberg, *The Great Reversal,* 50.
2 Darryl Hart, *From Billy Graham to Sarah Palin: Evangelicals and the Betrayal of American Conservatism* (Eerdmans Publishing Company, 2011), loc 388, 420, Kindle.
3 Ibid., loc 402-431.

post-World War II conservatism.[4] Evangelical attitudes on national policy were not fully developed or prioritized until the late 1970s. This instinctual political conservatism was not enough to keep progressives out until the rise of the more populist religious right.

From its inception, a door was opened to progressives within evangelicalism. Concerned that Christians were losing cultural relevance, Carl Henry, author of the 1947 book *The Uneasy Conscience of Modern Fundamentalism*, criticized fundamentalists for being "indifferent" to "social justice and international order."[5] Henry's book inspired progressives like Samuel Escobar and Richard Mouw to merge their social and political perspectives with their Christian faith.[6]

Harold Ockenga, the founding president of the National Association of Evangelicals, wrote the foreword to *Uneasy Conscience*. In it he recounted the story of a "Fundamentalist in faith" who "became a political liberal" on his "knees." Ockenga asserted that "if the Bible-believing Christian is on the wrong side of social problems such as war, race, class, labor, liquor, imperialism, etc. it is time to get over the fence to the right side," adding, "The church needs a progressive Fundamentalism with a social message."[7]

Ockenga became the first president of Fuller Theological Seminary, the premier academic institution of neo-evangelicalism, in 1947. In his dedication speech, he proposed a strategy to save the "Christian Culture of the West" from secularism by starting a "modern movement" to train young leaders to "redefine Christian thinking" and challenge unbelievers "in an intellectually respectable way" while positively influencing Christian denominations. Fuller became "the center of missions and evangelism on the basis of the gospel."[8]

In the face of a rising secular culture which placed a diminishing value on the authority of Christian clergy, the neo-evangelical strategy was to

---

4 Ibid., loc 107-108.
5 Henry, *The Uneasy Conscience of Modern Fundamentalism*, loc 157-158.
6 Swartz, *Moral Minority*, 133, 137.
7 Henry, *The Uneasy Conscience of Modern Fundamentalism*, loc 84-86.
8 Harold Ockenga, "The Challenge to the Christian Culture of the West," Fuller Theological Seminary, October 1, 1947. https://fullerstudio.fuller.edu/the-challenge-to-the-christian-culture-of-the-west-opening-convocation-october-1-1947.

train "powerful leaders" which "great nations" would be "keyed to."[9] In order to accomplish this goal, Fuller incrementally broadened its focus to include more than its initial course work in theology, philosophy, and apologetics by adopting priorities and disciplines thought to be more authoritative in a secular world.[10]

By 1972, the seminary prioritized "social concern" regarding: racial justice, "race relationships, problems of church and state, . . . social work, family guidance, care of handicapped children, . . . [problems in] urban society; the relationship between evangelism and social concern; concern for the oppressed and needy; . . . and the implications of the Gospel for Christian citizenship in contemporary society."[11] The success of seminaries like Fuller, and liberal arts schools like Wheaton College, attracted students and paved the way for other evangelical institutions to follow suit.[12] The stage was set for a new kind of social engagement.

Neo-evangelical leaders bequeathed to younger progressives a broader understanding of sin and of social responsibility which in turn allowed New Left ideas access into some quarters of mainstream evangelicalism. Words like "structural," "systemic," and "institutional," frequently used to describe sins and injustices in both mainline and progressive evangelical publications, became more common.

In the December 1972 edition of *World Vision* magazine, former NAE president Paul Rees stated that conversions alone were not adequate in challenging "structured social evils." As an example, Rees cited the fact that it took "saved and unsaved . . . cobelligerents" to end slavery, even though many

---

9 Henry, *The Uneasy Conscience of Modern Fundamentalism*, loc 528-529, 534-535, 546.
10 Fuller Theological Seminary, "Catalog: Academic Year 1947-1948," *Academic Catalogs*, 1947. https://digitalcommons.fuller.edu/academic_catalogs/12; David Wells, *No Place for Truth: Or Whatever Happened to Evangelical Theology?* (Wm. B. Eerdmans Publishing, 1994), 171.
11 Fuller Theological Seminary, "Catalog: School of Theology and School of World Mission, Academic Year 1970-1972," *Academic Catalogs*, 1970. https://digitalcommons.fuller.edu/academic_catalogs/12
12 For more on Fuller's extensive influence in evangelicalism see Quebedeaux, *The Young Evangelicals: Revolution in Orthodoxy*, 71-72; FitzGerald, *The Evangelicals*, 259.

slaveholders were Christians. He quoted George Johnson, dean of Religious Studies at McGill University, who said the gospel should address pollution, nuclear weapons, and civil rights. He also referenced James Sheror, Professor of World Mission at the Lutheran School of Theology, who stated that salvation had "social and political, as well as psychic and personal, dimensions."[13] Like many evangelical elites, Rees already accommodated the rationale progressives appealed to in drafting the Chicago Declaration and it came as no surprise when he signed it the following year.

Besides Paul Rees, Carl Henry, and Foy Valentine, several other mainstream evangelicals also signed the 1973 Chicago Declaration including Bernard Ramm, who taught at the California Baptist Theological Seminary, Joseph Bayly, former head of InterVarsity Press and columnist for *Eternity* magazine, Frank Gaebelein, co-editor of *Christianity Today*, and chairman of the style committee of the New International Version of the Bible, Vernon Grounds, former president of the Evangelical Theological Society and president of Denver Seminary, Stephen Charles Mott, professor of Christian Social Ethics at Gordon-Conwell Theological Seminary, and Lewis Smedes, department chairman in theology and ethics at Fuller. Even Billy Graham, when he declined to sign, told *Christianity Today*, "I think we have to identify with the changing of structures in society and try to do our part."[14]

Billy Graham, however, did not hesitate to sign the Lausanne Covenant presented at the 1974 Lausanne International Congress on World Evangelization. Graham framed the event as specifically focused on evangelization. He declared: "We're enthusiastic about all the many things Churches properly do from worship to social concern. But our calling is to a specific sector of the church's responsibility: Evangelism."[15] Yet, along

---

13 Paul Rees, "Will Bangkok Be a Watershed or a Washout?" *World Vision Magazine*, December 1972, 23.

14 Carl Henry, "The Gospel and Society," *Christianity Today*, Accessed March 3, 2020. https://www.christianitytoday.com/ct/1974/september-13/footnotes-gospel-and-society.html.

15 *Let the Earth Hear His Voice*, directed by Michael Hooser, (World Wide Pictures, 1974), 9:40, https://www.lausanne.org/content/documentary-about-1974-congress.

with other mainstream evangelical voices, such as Francis Schaeffer and Carl Henry, Graham signed the covenant which included a statement expressing "penitence" for neglecting "social concern." The statement made a careful distinction between "political liberation" and "salvation" by framing "socio-political involvement" as "necessary" since the "message of salvation implies a message of judgement upon . . . alienation, oppression, and discrimination."[16] By lifting social action to the point of including it in a conference on evangelism, neo-evangelicals showed they prioritized it far more than fundamentalists.

The evangelical left's shared disagreement with fundamentalist's individualized gospel helped gain a measure of acceptance for progressives within neo-evangelicalism.[17] In the 1960s, Wheaton faculty such as Ozzie Edwards, who contributed to the *Cross and the Flag* and *The Other Side,* J. Edward Hakes, who was active in liberal politics, as well as sociologist Ka Tong Gaw and John Alexander, all "emerged as campus leaders on civil rights."[18] Fuller Theological Seminary's board of trustees not only included Billy Graham, but also William Pannell, who rejected "old style evangelism" that did not meet "human needs," and believed the "conservative brand of Christianity" associated with "American patriotism, free enterprise, and the Republican party" was perpetuating "the myth of white supremacy."[19] Fuller was not the only neo-evangelical entity to platform young progressives.

---

16 "The Lausanne Covenant."

17 In *The Fundamentals* (1910-1915), Charles Trumbull, editor of the *Sunday School Times,* warned against "The salvation of society regardless of the salvation of the individual . . ." taking his cue from Billy Sunday who preached "the individual Gospel" and said "little about social service," while "revolutionizing" communities. Princeton professor Charles Erdman opposed the "social gospel," instead promoting "the social principles of Christ" related to "marriage and family," "the stewardship of wealth," the responsibilities of "masters and servants" and "employers and employees," as well as the "the sacredness of the state" and "duties of Christian citizenship." Erdman maintained that "the hope of the world" was "not in a new social order" but in "a kingdom established by Christ." See R.A. Torrey, et al., *The Fundamentals - A Testimony to the Truth,* Vol. 3. Rio, WI: (AGES Software, 2000), 87-88, 90; Vol. 4, 87-88, 90.

18 Randall Balmer, 317; Swartz, *Moral Minority,* 31, 195.

19 Quebedeaux, *The Young Evangelicals,* 71; Swartz, *Moral Minority,* loc 675, Kindle Edition; William Pannell, *My Friend, the Enemy* (Word Books, 1968), 53.

The most prominent evangelical para-church organization to open its doors to the evangelical left was InterVarsity Christian Fellowship, a prominent campus ministry which represented 26,000 students by 1977.[20] The organization produced "pro-civil rights books, magazines, and sermons" throughout the 1970s.[21] Samuel Escobar served as the ministry's general director in Canada, John Perkins spoke multiple times at InterVarsity's Urbana Youth Leadership conferences throughout the 1970s and 80s, and William Pannell and Tom Skinner gained deep influence within the organization.[22]

In 1970, the campus ministry hosted its major Urbana conference with 12,000 in attendance. The theme was, "Christ the Liberator." Leighton Ford, who was an associate of Billy Graham and proponent of "revolutionary evangelism," which involved service projects as well as "affirmative action" and "War on Poverty efforts," spoke.[23] John Stott, the "chief architect" of the Lausanne Covenant, also spoke. Before the keynote address from Tom Skinner entitled "Racism and World Evangelism," Soul Liberation played a black power song called "Power to the People."[24] Skinner then denounced "Americanism," the "police," which he maintained were "nothing more than the occupational force in the black community for maintaining the interests of white society," as well as "1% of the total population [which] controls the entire economic system." In contrast, Skinner promoted the "revolutionary" Jesus who was arrested for coming "to change the system."[25]

Even organizations like Campus Crusade for Christ (CCC), led by Bill Bright, a very patriotic and deeply anti-communist graduate of Fuller, spoke the

---

20 Keith Hunt, and Gladys Hunt, *For Christ and the University: The Story of InterVarsity Christian Fellowship of the USA - 1940-1990* (InterVarsity Press, 2009), 306.
21 Swartz, "The Evangelical Left and the Politicization of Evangelicalism," 276.
22 "Samuel Escobar Peruvian Missiologist and Missionary to the US and Spain," *InterVarsity Urbana Student Missions Conference*," InterVarsity, Urbana Student Missions Conference, 2003. https://urbana.org/bio/samuel-escobar; Marsh, 5; Swartz, *Moral Minority*, 34.
23 Quebedeaux, *The Young Evangelicals*, 88-89.
24 Edward Gilbreath, "A Prophet Out of Harlem," *Christianity Today*, September 16, 1996.
25 Tom Skinner, "The U.S. Racial Crisis and World Evangelism," Urbana Student Missions Conference, 1970. https://urbana.org/message/us-racial-crisis-and-world-evangelism.

language of the counter culture at times in order to get their message out. CCC speakers talked "about the revolutionary impact of Jesus Christ." In counter demonstrations against the "New Left" or "antiwar activity," students and staff sported signs like, "'Spiritual Reality in Jesus Christ,' 'Students Denouncing Sin,' . . . 'Boycott Hell! Accept Jesus,'" or 'Jesus is a Revolutionary.'"[26] The Christian World Liberation Front at Berkeley, which existed to "introduce people to the revolutionary program" in which "Jesus Christ" would "build a movement . . . personally humane and politically sound," initially grew out of a CCC chapter.[27]

Despite this cross pollination, most mainstream evangelicals did not fully accept New Left solutions to systemic injustice since both they, and their fundamentalist parents, placed a high priority on civil order and respect for authority. While Billy Graham affirmed "a social aspect of the Gospel" which addressed hunger and disease, he also claimed his ministry represented the "Kingdom of God" which, as exemplified by Jesus and Paul, did not authorize political demonstration.[28] Remaining obedient to biblical teaching on hierarchy and maintaining cultural respectability placed limits on the extent to which neo-evangelicals would go in order to effect structural change.

Leading up to the 1970s, most evangelicals were also more concerned about communism and materialism than they were about "racial, class, and gender discrimination." Even on these issues, though, the church's job was not to "reform society or engage in political activism." Instead, they believed "the health of a free society depended on a virtuous people."[29] Neo-evangelicals, like Carl Henry and Harold Ockenga, made cultivating virtuous leadership a major goal.[30] Even though this focus on creating leaders in the secular world allowed for a rationale which justified New Left influenced Christianity,

---

26 John Turner, *Bill Bright and Campus Crusade for Christ: The Renewal of Evangelicalism in Postwar America*, (University of North Carolina Press, 2009), 127.
27 "New Berkeley Liberation Program," *Right On*, July 1969.
28 Andrew Finstuen, Anne Wills, and Grant Wacker, *Billy Graham: American Pilgrim*, (Oxford University Press, 2017), 128; William Martin, *A Prophet with Honor: The Billy Graham Story*, (Zondervan, 2018), 192.
29 Hart, *From Billy Graham to Sarah Palin*, loc 367-371, 336-337.
30 Swartz, *Moral Minority*, 21.

neo-evangelical leaders still rejected most of the social reform movements which emerged in the 1960s.

Billy Graham was friends with Richard Nixon, took a gradualist approach to integration, and taught in 1969 that "the policeman is an agent and servant of God" with a "tremendous responsibility at this hour of revolution and anarchy and rebellion against all authority that is sweeping across our nation."[31] Harold Ockenga supported both Richard Nixon and the Vietnam War while believing "The United States of America" had "been assigned a destiny comparable to ancient Israel."[32] The premier evangelical magazine, *Christianity Today*, "counseled patience" on "the Civil Rights movement," "supported the war in Vietnam and championed individualism and economic freedom over against collectivist views."[33]

Neo-evangelicals may have opened the door for progressives, but they certainly did not open it all the way. The evangelical left was too absolute in their proposals, too immediate in their desired implementation, and too unconcerned about their reputation. In short, their disposition was more than a little similar to the fundamentalists which neo-evangelicals were trying to separate themselves from.

---

31 Edward Fiske, "The Closest Thing To A White House Chaplain," *The New York Times*, June 8, 1969. https://archive.nytimes.com/www.nytimes.com/books/97/07/06/reviews/graham-magazine.html.
32 Rosell, 12.
33 Steensland and Goff, *The New Evangelical Social Engagement*, 268.

CHAPTER THIRTEEN
FUNDAMENTALISM REBORN

IF THERE IS ANYTHING PROGRESSIVE evangelicals were against, besides the "oppressive" "American system," it was a conservative brand of evangelicalism known as fundamentalism.[1] Because religious fundamentalism tried to solve issues like "the race problem" by changing attitudes alone, instead of social structures directly, evangelicals influenced by New Left thinking rejected its approach to social reform.[2] Jim Wallis characterized "fundamentalist proof-texting" as advocating "conservative, militarist, patriotic, racist, and sexist distortions of the Bible."[3] Letha Scanzoni thought fundamentalists used "scripture to keep any group back."[4] Richard Mouw praised neo-evangelicals for "attempting to lead" fundamentalists "away from bitterness and isolation and toward a responsible intellectual and cultural engagement."[5]

In *The Fundamentals* (1910-1915), from which fundamentalists receive their name, Charles Trumbull, editor of the *Sunday School Times*, warned against "The salvation of society regardless of the salvation of the individual." Trumbull identified Billy Sunday as an example of an evangelist who preached "the individual Gospel" and said "little about social service," while

---

1 Jim Wallis, "Post-American Christianity," *Sojourners*, September 1, 1971. https://sojo.net/magazine/fall-1971/post-american-christianity.
2 Art Gish, "The New Left and Christian Radicalism," *Sojourners*, September 1, 1971. https://sojo.net/magazine/fall-1971/new-left-and-christian-radicalism.
3 Jim Wallis, "Idols Closer to Home," *Sojourners*, May 1, 1979. https://sojo.net/magazine/may-1979/idols-closer-home.
4 Janene Putman,"An Interview with Letha Dawson Scanzoni."
5 Richard Mouw, "Sexual Politics," *Sojourners*, August 1, 1974. https://sojo.net/magazine/august-september-1974/sexual-politics.

"revolutionizing" communities. Like Trumbell and Sunday, Princeton professor Charles Erdman opposed the "social gospel," instead promoting "the social principles of Christ" related to "marriage and family," "the stewardship of wealth," the responsibilities of "masters and servants" and "employers and employees," as well as the "the sacredness of the state" and "duties of Christian citizenship." Erdman maintained that "the hope of the world" was "not in a new social order" but in "a kingdom established by Christ."[6]

Because of its individualistic focus, Carl Henry and other neo-evangelicals described fundamentalism as "the modern priest and Levite, by-passing suffering humanity" with a "gospel that is indifferent to the needs of the total nor of the global man."[7] According to George Marsden, early twentieth century fundamentalism, itself a reaction against theological liberalism and the social gospel, also had a "sectarian, inward-looking, anti-intellectual, and antisocial" tendency in contrast to the nineteen century Northern social reform movements which preceded it.[8] In 1976, Harold Ockenga differentiated evangelicalism from fundamentalism based on "its repudiation of separatism," engagement with "the theological dialogue of the day," and "emphasis upon the application of the gospel to the sociological, political, and economic areas of life."[9]

Despite the chasm existing between fundamentalists and progressive evangelicals on social engagement, both groups shared a certain uncompromising posture absent from their theological cousins, the neo-evangelicals. A dualistic attitude, a propensity toward separatism, a habit of pressuring members to keep extra-biblical precepts, a reputation known for what it was against, and a willingness to sacrifice social approval, all characterized both traditions. Though most of these features were also shared with the secular "New Left," it is likely that many progressive Christians were also shaped by their fundamentalist backgrounds.

---

6 R.A. Torrey, et al., *The Fundamentals - A Testimony to the Truth*, Vol. 3., 87-88, 90; Vol. 4, 87-88, 90.

7 Henry, *The Uneasy Conscience of Modern Fundamentalism*, loc 315, 107.

8 George Marsden, *Reforming Fundamentalism: Fuller Seminary and the New Evangelicalism* (William B. Eerdmans Publishing Company, 1995), 146, 94.

9 Harold Lindsell, *The Battle for the Bible* (Zondervan Publishing House, 1976), 11.

Jim Wallis, William Pannell, Sharon Gallagher, John Alexander, Richard Mouw, Wes Granberg-Michaelson, Stephen Charles Mott, Richard Quebedeaux, Virginia Ramey Mollenkott, Orlando Costas, and many other members of the evangelical left were deeply connected to fundamentalism during their early years.[10]

In 1976, Thomas Finger observed what he described as "Neo-fundamentalists" who "criticize society . . . from the left" and "reject fundamentalism, but retain its dualistic attitudes." Their interpretation of Jesus' "uncompromising stance" translated into "indignant protest, devoid of compassion and sensitivity."[11] Nineteen years earlier, Carl Henry had similarly described "much of" fundamentalist "leadership" as exhibiting "a harsh temperament, a spirit of lovelessness and strife."[12] Certainly, the attitude Finger and Henry depict did not characterize either movement in its entirety. Yet, certain prominent spokesman for both groups became known for their negative rhetoric. There is little doubt that many progressive evangelicals observed this puritanical posture flowing from the tradition of their fundamentalist parents and grandparents. In the broader culture, fundamentalists became known for such attitudes.

Colorful preachers, like John Roach Straton in New York City, helped create a stereotypical fundamentalist mold for years to come. In his 1918 sermon, "Will New York Be Destroyed if it Does not Repent?" Straton "attacked the vice, gluttony, gaming, and indecency of New York's hotels and cabarets, comparing the city with Nineveh, Babylon, Sodom, [and] Gomorrah."[13] This emphasis became a mainstay within the tradition. Wes Granberg-Michaelson described the 1960s "Fundamentalist movement" he grew up in as a culture where "no one smoked, drank alcohol, went to movies, used playing cards, spoke profanity, or danced. We didn't even talk about sex. We believed in Jesus, and we believed in America—the Republican version."[14] Social taboos, like drinking,

10 Jim Wallis, "A Conversation with Young Evangelicals," *Sojourners*, January 1, 1975. https://sojo. net/magazine/january-1975/conversation-young-evangelicals; Swartz, *Moral Minority*, 21.
11 Finger, "Reformed/Anabaptist Conversation: Jesus as Ethical Norm."
12 Carl Henry, *Evangelical Responsibility in Contemporary Theology*, Pathway Books, A Series of Contemporary Evangelical Studies, (Eerdmans, 1957), 43.
13 George Marsden, *Fundamentalism and American Culture*, (Oxford University Press, 2006), 162.
14 Granberg-Michaelson, *Unexpected Destinations*, loc 648, 323-324.

dancing, playing cards, and attending theaters were not only morally re-stricted behaviors for believers, but also the source material for fundamental-ist preachers' attacks on worldiness.[15] However, personal vice was not the only thing fundamentalists opposed.

After the second world war especially, fundamentalists like Carl McIntire focused much of their energy into opposing Marxism. McIntire, a fiery radio preacher, chastised the Federal Council of Churches for trying to implement "love . . . benevolence and stewardship" through a "social program" forwarded by legislation "and the cooperative action of society, rather than by the power of the Gospel in the hearts of men."[16] When the Council adopted "The Cleveland Declaration" in 1945, which stated that "the right to private property is not an absolute right but a right qualified by the public interest," McIntire responded by claiming that the "Ten Commandments" were "the eternal bill of rights of the individual" and that "any organization . . . that would attack the right of private property [was] attacking the eternal truth of God."[17]

In 1972, McIntire denounced Richard Nixon's attempts to de-escalate the Cold War by transporting "two busloads full of protesters . . . to Miami Beach, Florida, the site of the Republican Party convention." He described "Communists" as characterized by "abysmal depravity," "no responsibility to God," and "inspired by demonic powers."[18] Other fundamentalists like "Fred Schwartz . . . and Billy James Hargis, [also] specialized in anti-communism."[19] Even Billy Graham had sat on the board for Eisenhower's anti-communist Foundation for Religious Action in the Social and Civil Order along with other

---

15 Quebedeaux, *The Young Evangelicals*, 22.

16 Gladys Rhoads and Nancy Anderson, *McIntire: Defender of Faith and Freedom* (Xulon Press, Incorporated, 2012), 102-105; The Federal Council of Churches changed its name to the National Council of Churches in 1950; Carl McIntire, *Twentieth Century Reformation* (Christian Beacon Press, 1946), 140.

17 Carl McIntire, *The Rise of the Tyrant: Controlled Economy Vs. Private Enterprise*, Henry Ford Estate Collection (Christian Beacon Press, 1945), 65, 15.

18 Markku Ruotsila, *Fighting Fundamentalist: Carl McIntire and the Politicization of American Fundamentalism* (Oxford University Press, 2016), 235.

19 George Marsden, *Fundamentalism and American Culture: The Shaping of Twentieth Century Evangelicalism, 1870-1925*, American Studies Collection (Oxford University Press, 1980), 232.

Protestants, Catholics, and Jews.[20] Early in his ministry, he would occasionally describe the Soviet system as "master-minded by Satan" or "demon-possessed."[21]

This kind of absolute terminology was frequently called upon by progressive evangelicals in order to describe threats they believed came from the opposite side of the political debate. America was like "Satan," a "wolf in sheep's clothing," and "one of the greatest perpetrators of violence and exploitation in the world."[22] The status quo of "existing, usual, or traditional views, habits, conditions, or methods," was part of the "kingdom of Satan."[23] Richard Nixon was a "symbol of the arrogant, self-righteous, imperial spirit that has shaped American history."[24] American foreign policy was an "ugly record" of "interventionism."[25] The Vietnam War was "a national sin and disgrace."[26] Members of the evangelical left used the term "demonic" to characterize everything from objects, like "money and riches" and "American war machinery," to ideas, such as modern humanity's "ingenuity" in creating weapons, and "economic or political interests" used "to justify . . . intimidation, repression, and torture." Social injustices like "poverty" and apartheid, as well as the attitudes that caused them, such as "native ethnocentrism" were also "demonic."[27] Historian David Swartz observes that the

---

20 Fitzgerald, *The Evangelicals*, 185.

21 Martin, *A Prophet With Honor*, 167; Fitzgerald, *The Evangelicals*, 180.

22 Bill Lane, "Lessons from Vietnam," *Sojourners*, March 1, 1973. https://sojo.net/magazine/march-april-1973/lessons-vietnam.

23 Bill Lane, "The Christian Radical," *Sojourners*, October 1, 1974. https://sojo.net/magazine/october-1974/christian-radical.

24 Jim Wallis, "The New Regime," *Sojourners*, October 1, 1974 https://sojo.net/magazine/october-1974/new-regime.

25 Wallis, *The New Radical*, 49

26 Wallis, *Revive Us Again*, 16.

27 John Burkholder,"Money," *Sojourners*, December 1, 1974. https://sojo.net/magazine/december-1974/money; Charles Fager, "Ethics, Principalities and Nonviolence," *Sojourners*, November 1, 1974, https://sojo.net/magazine/november-1974/ethics-principalities-and-nonviolence; John Howard Yoder, "Living the Disarmed Life." *Sojourners*, May 1, 1977, https://sojo.net/magazine/may-1977/living-disarmed-life; Wes Granberg-Michaelson, "Suffering with the Victims," *Sojourners*, July 1, 1976. https://sojo.net/magazine/july-august-1976/suffering-victims; Philip Amerson, "Excess or Access?," *Sojourners*, July 1, 1979. https://sojo.net/magazine/july-1979/excess-or-access; Clarence Hillard, "A Dissent to the Covenant Issued at the International Congress on World Evangelization," *Sojourners*, November 1, 1974. https://sojo.net/magazine/november-1974/dissent-covenant-issued-in-ternational-congress-world-evangelization; John Howard Yoder,"The Biblical Mandate," *Sojourners*, April 1, 1974. https://sojo.net/magazine/april-1974/biblical-mandate.

Jim Wallis led Post-Americans "began to sound more like their fundamentalist grandparents than their neo-evangelical parents in their abundant use of apocalyptic language."[28] Neutrality was not an option.

Ron Sider's belief in personal responsibility for systemic sin exemplified this puritanical attitude well. He maintained that "if one is involved in unjust social structures," which included realities as seemingly inescapable as benefitting from "international trade patterns," and "does nothing to try to change them, then one is personally guilty in the same way that one is guilty if one commits an act of adultery or tells a lie."[29] From the pages of the *Post-American* in 1972, Art Gish excoriated the neo-evangelical posture of trying to "fit into middle-class society and gain respectability" while failing to talk "about sin." With a tip of the hat to fundamentalists, Gish declared, "the radicals" were "correct in saying that in order to affirm, one must first negate" just as "the old time preachers said the same when they maintained that in order to say yes to Christ one must say no to Satan." Jim Wallis' mentor, Clark Pinnock, summed up the sentiment when he stated:

> The battle for justice turns out to require even more than the regeneration of individuals and more than the transformation of societal structures. It has the proportions of a spiritual battle of cosmic dimensions against spiritual powers which are seeking to enslave human life and hold us all in misery and bondage. Behind the human agents identified with the forces of wickedness, there is a demonic presence which must be confronted too.[30]

Young progressives, like fundamentalists before them, assumed a necessarily dualistic ideology of good or evil which translated into a negative and combative posture.

---

28 Swartz, *Moral Minority*, 63.
29 Williams, *The Weakness of Evangelical Ethics*, 4-5.
30 Clark Pinnock, "An Evangelical Theology of Human Liberation, Part II," *Sojourners*, March 1, 1976. https://sojo.net/magazine/march-1976/evangelical-theology-human-liberation-part-ii.

In order to confront worldly and demonic forces, progressive evangelicals, like their secular New Left counterparts, raised awareness against social injustice. Interestingly, Art Gish noticed similarities between the "methods . . . found in the civil rights and peace movements, and the fundamentalist movement." While admitting that he "used to make fun of the fundamentalists for their street preaching, handing out tracts, and door-to-door visitation," Gish knew that he was using the exact same methods for proclaiming "liberation" from "slavery, oppression, and exploitation." He noted that "the content may have changed, but the form was the same!"[31] Interestingly, some fundamentalists also engaged in a version of political activism, though they did not conflate it with spreading the message of the gospel.

For example, on the issue of the Vietnam War, fundamentalists like John Rice, a Baptist pastor and editor of the fundamentalist periodical, *The Sword of the Lord*, declared that American troops "would be carrying out the command of God."[32] Carl McIntire organized rallies to support the war like his 1971 "March for Victory." He maintained, "It is the message of the infallible Bible that gives men the right to participate in such conflicts, and to do it with the realization that God is for them, that God will help them."[33] Such sentiments reflected the influence of nineteenth century Northern revivalism and the Puritan concept of a national covenant.[34] During World War I, Billy Sunday had affirmed, "Christianity and Patriotism are synonymous terms and hell and traitors are synonymous."[35] Fundamentalists accepted the notion that the United States was the beneficiary of divine blessing, and, by extension, virtuous.

---

31 Art Gish, "Reconsideration," *Sojourners*, June 1, 1972. https://sojo.net/magazine/summer-1972/reconsideration.
32 Swartz, *Moral Minority*, loc 797.
33 Angela Lahr, *Millennial Dreams and Apocalyptic Nightmares: The Cold War Origins of Political Evangelicalism*, (Oxford University Press, USA, 2007), 182.
34 Puritan John Winthrop, in his famous "City on a Hill" speech entitled, "A Model of Christian Charity," stated, "Thus stands the cause between God and us. We are entered into covenant with Him for this work." See John Winthrop, "A Model of Christian Charity," *The Winthrop Society*, 1630. https://www.winthropsociety.com/doc_charity.php.
35 George Marsden, *Understanding Fundamentalism and Evangelicalism*, (Eerdmans Publishing Company, 1991), 51.

Fundamentalists also believed American culture was in danger of breaking its covenant with God by engaging in moral vice. Therefore, it was incumbent on Christians to be "salt and light" by opposing vice and promoting virtue. God judged the national character in much the same way He judged personal character. Evil came from sinful hearts, and it was man's prerogative to make a decision to follow Christ and reject sinful behavior. On a grand scale, this positive move was referred to as a "revival." Fundamentalists made reviving America a major goal.

In addition to false religions and foreign opposition, the enemies of revival took the form of certain domestic businesses and industries. Hollywood and theaters, casinos and gambling, bars and alcohol, and dance halls, with their sexually provocative displays, all sought to corrupt the moral values and civic virtue of American culture.[36] During the first half of the twentieth century, as fundamentalism traveled to the South and atheistic Communism became an increased threat, a simultaneous reverence for the military came to characterize the tradition.[37] In the minds of fundamentalists, certain human associations and institutions within American culture were participating in a cosmic spiritual war for the soul and direction of the country. Progressive evangelicals shared this fear, though they believed the different organizational structures were to blame.

The evangelical left promoted an extra-biblical vice list, which, unlike their parents,' was more abstract in its focus on systemic oppression. Instead of drinking and playing cards, young progressives vilified mind-sets such as the "desire to have more," make a "profit," and devote oneself to "tradition" for tradition's sake. Even passively endorsing "militarism," "imperialism," or "waste," through inaction, meant complicity.[38] Members of the evangelical

---

36 George Marsden cites a D.L. Moody sermon on "Temptation" as a "characteristic example" of a fundamentalist vice list. The "four great temptations" were "the theater," "disregard of the Sabbath," "Sunday newspapers," and "atheistic teachings, including evolution." See Marsden, *Fundamentalism and American Culture*, 35.

37 Marsden, *Fundamentalism and American Culture*, 240.

38 Peter Davids, "God and Mammon In the Early Church," *Sojourners*, March 1, 1978. https://sojo.net/magazine/march-1978/god-and-mammon-early-church; Art Gish, "The New Left and Christian Radicalism," *Sojourners*, September 1, 1971. https://sojo.

left often used the term "sin" to describe a complex state of affairs involving different participants at various levels. For example, in 1973, Mark Hatfield called the Vietnam War a "sin that has scarred the national soul" during the "21st National Prayer Breakfast."[39] Oftentimes, progressive evangelicals appealed to the concept of idolatry as a way of qualifying New Left concepts as sins. Ed Guinan, an "active member of the Community for Creative Non-Violence in Washington, D.C.," described "the idolatrous" as those who elevated things like "property" and "security" above human lives.[40] Jim Wallis spoke about "political power," which, along with military might was routinely described using the term.[41] In fact, everything from "nuclear weapons," to male headship, to "flags and borders" were categorized as "idolatries of the social and political order."[42]

Evangelicals, who accepted New Left critiques of American society, believed the kingdom of God was in a state of conflict with the nation. Mark Hatfield thought it "dangerous" to "merge piety with . . . patriotism."[43] John Perkins believed "cultural values like . . . patriotism" "nullified" Christian witness.[44] Jim Wallis wrote, "The determination of the movemental church is to be those of a

net/magazine/fall-1971/new-left-and-christian-radicalism; John Stott, "The Conservative Radical," *Sojourners*, November 1, 1973. https://sojo.net/magazine/november-december-1973/conservative-radical; Jim Wallis, "Post-American Christianity," *Sojourners*, September 1, 1971. https://sojo.net/magazine/fall-1971/post-american-christianity.

39 James Wooten, "Nixon Hears War Called a 'Sin,'" *The New York Times*, February 2, 1973, sec. Archives. https://www.nytimes.com/1973/02/02/archives/nixon-hears-war-called-a-sin.html.

40 Ed Guinan, "In Communion with Trampled Bodies," *Sojourners*, April 1, 1975. https://sojo.net/magazine/april-1975/communion-trampled-bodies.

41 Jim Wallis, "The Move to Washington, D.C." *Sojourners*, August 1, 1975. https://sojo.net/magazine/august-september-1975/move-washington-dc; David Osielski, "Senator Mark Hatfield Advocates 'Power of Love,'" *Wheaton Record* 96, no. 14 (February 15, 1974). https://recollections.wheaton.edu/2018/03/senator-mark-hatfield-advocates-power-of-love/; Jim Wallis, "The Boston Affirmations," *Sojourners*, February 1, 1976. https://sojo.net/magazine/february-1976/boston-affirmations.

42 Henri Nouwen, "Letting Go of All Things," *Sojourners*, May 1, 1979. https://sojo.net/magazine/may-1979/letting-go-all-things; Mollenkott, "Women and the Bible," *Sojourners*, February 1, 1976, https://sojo.net/magazine/february-1976/women-and-bible; Jim Forest, "There Was Always Bread," *Sojourners*, December 1, 1976. https://sojo.net/magazine/december-1976/there-was-always-bread; Jim Wallis, "Many to Belief, but Few to Obedience," *Sojourners*, March 1, 1976. https://sojo.net/magazine/march-1976/many-belief-few-obedience.

43 Gasaway, *Progressive Evangelicals and the Pursuit of Social Justice*, 38.

44 John Perkins, "The Reconciled Community in a World at War," *Sojourners*, July 1, 1977. https://sojo.net/magazine/july-1977/reconciled-community-world-war.

new order who live by the values and ethical priorities of Jesus Christ and His Kingdom in the midst of the indifference and injustice of the American church and state."[45] Since all structures of the American "system" were tainted with the "corrupt values" of the "culture," the Post-Americans dedicated themselves "to no ideology, government, or system, but to active obedience to" the "Lord and His Kingdom."[46] Yet, in doing so, they, once again, mimicked the otherworldly and separatistic pattern set forth by fundamentalists.

Both fundamentalists and progressive evangelicals had an affinity for separating from, and often vilifying, others who deviated from what neo-evangelicals considered to be secondary issues. Sometimes they criticized and shunned people for merely associating with someone who had violated religious taboos. One letter to the editor of *Christianity Today* complained that if Jim Wallis "could only muster the same sort of sweet openness toward the members of Christ's body with whom he disagrees . . . he might then make a unifying contribution. Until that time he can expect to produce little but strife."[47] In general, fundamentalists held rigid views on doctrinal issues while progressive evangelicals held rigid views on political issues. The way both groups treated Billy Graham is illustrative of this phenomena.

Throughout most of his ministry, Billy Graham held to standard evangelical understandings of core Christian doctrines related to sin, judgment, salvation, and Christ. He also favored anti-communism, patriotism, and a gradualist approach to integration. There was enough moderation and variety in Graham's political views to afford him the friendships of both conservatives and progressive presidents. Yet, many fundamentalists and progressive evangelicals were very critical of him. Carl McIntire, Bob Jones, and John Rice all denounced Graham for his "ecumenicism," demonstrated by his partnership with mainline denominations in the 1957 New York Crusade, his affiliation with the National Association

---

45 Jim Wallis, "What Is the People's Christian Coalition," *Sojourners,* September 1, 1972. https://sojo.net/magazine/fall-1972/what-peoples-christian-coalition.
46 Ibid.
47 "Eutychus and His Kin: August 16, 1974," *Christianity Today,* August 16, 1974.

of Evangelicals, and his participation at the 1966 World Congress on Evangelism in Berlin, which instructed speakers to "avoid attacking communism."[48]

Evangelicals on the Left likewise accused Graham of being unwilling to confess the sins of America.[49] His friendship with Nixon especially hurt his image with progressives. Donald Dayton, the husband of Lucille Sider Dayton and author of *Discovering an Evangelical Heritage,* believed Graham failed to use his friendship with Nixon to stop bombing in Vietnam.[50] The editors of the *Post-American* compared Richard Nixon and Billy Graham to "Old Testament kings and priests" who approved of the "hypocrisy of false worship." There was no mistaking who Mark Hatfield was referring to when he warned of the threat of "idolatry" to "the god of an American civil religion," right in front of both President Nixon and Billy Graham.[51] Author Brantley Gasaway points out that "no one seemed more implicated in civil religion than Billy Graham." The reason "*Post-American* authors rebuked Graham" was not just for associating with the President or businessmen, "but also for urging Christians to honor America."[52]

Rigid and often extra-biblical and extra-confessional standards erected barriers for participation in both movements. These tests of fellowship catalyzed the formation of cultural ghettos in which the faithful, convinced of their specific remedies and standards, launched efforts to conform the broader Christian and secular cultures to their mold through conversion. Fundamentalists geared their institutional efforts almost entirely toward biblical instruction and church ministry as seen in the Bible institute model. Progressive evangelicals focused their attention on biblical living by forming radical communities. The former was characterized by pastors, tradition, and knowledge, while the latter was marked by political prophets, progression, and

48 Martin, *A Prophet With Honor,* 226, 223, 340.
49 Dale Brown, "Revolutionary Implications of the Atonement," *Sojourners,* May 1, 1973. https://sojo.net/magazine/may-june-1973/revolutionary-implications-atonement.
50 Donald Dayton, *Discovering an Evangelical Heritage,* (Harper & Row, 1976), 8.
51 The Editors,"Signs of a New Order," *Sojourners,* March 1, 1973, https://sojo.net/magazine/march-april-1973/signs-new-order.
52 Gasaway, *Progressive Evangelicals and the Pursuit of Social Justice,* (University of North Carolina Press, 2014), 38.

feeling. However, both groups necessarily excluded competing groups. At the same time, their mission was to compel all members from other groups to disband and join theirs. Historian Darryl Hart notes that Richard Mouw's "vision of community" actually "depended on a form of separatism assumed in the old bogeyman: fundamentalism."[53]

Hart also observes that like "their parents and grandparents," "evangelical critics of conservatism" believed "politics was still basically a matter of doing God's will, and the criteria for public policy and just rule continued to be the goal of avoiding worldliness."[54] For fundamentalists, worldliness meant participation in concrete sinful actions which undermined Christian and American values. For progressive evangelicals, worldliness was understood as demonstrating complicity with the status quo of unjust American values since America was not in danger of falling, but was, in Jim Wallis' words, already "a fallen nation."[55] With similar motivation, both fundamentalists and progressives opposed the world and sought to work toward the establishment of the kingdom of God. The major difference between them was found in their understanding of what "the world" represented in contrast with the "kingdom."

If fundamentalists were guilty of practicing "civil religion," progressive evangelicals practiced something very similar. John Alexander thought Christians "must fulfill their responsibilities in the state and not isolate themselves."[56] From the pages of the *Post-American*, founding member Bob Sabath wrote that biblical doctrine included "crucial," critically significant, "important," and necessary "political implications."[57] Jim Wallis believed it was "essential" for Christians to "study . . . economic, political, social, and cultural realities" so they could take "political action."[58] Young progressives habitually protested, voted, and peti-

53 Hart, *From Billy Graham to Sarah Palin*, loc 630.
54 Ibid., 633-635.
55 Wallis, "Biblical Politics."
56 Gasaway, *Progressive Evangelicals and the Pursuit of Social Justice*, 30.
57 Bob Sabath, "Emily Post and Richard Nixon Revisited." *Sojourners*, March 1, 1972. https://sojo.net/magazine/spring-1972/emily-post-and-richard-nixon-revisited.
58 Jim Wallis, "The New Community," *Sojourners*, September 1, 1973, https://sojo.net/magazine/september-october-1973/new-community.

tioned civil leaders to make decisions in conformity with their agenda. Political involvement was part of both "evangelistic responsibility" and "worship."[59]

Because politics was so central to the mission of young evangelicals, they were actually more focused on influencing the government than fundamentalists and neo-evangelicals were. However, their efforts to change "the system" fell under the umbrella of exerting a "prophetic voice," a concept which saturated much of their literature. In 1975, Clark Pinnock described "new evangelicals" as speaking "prophetically to society and to power while restructuring its own life by the standard of the kingdom." In a 1978 interview for *Christianity Today*, Charles Peter Wagner, a pioneer of the church growth movement and professor at Fuller, described "*Sojourners, The Other Side,* people like Ron Sider" as "prophets" for confronting the "arrogance" of "majority culture."[60] Because young progressives were able to think of themselves as outsiders, in the template of an Old Testament prophet, they perceived their quest for a just "social and political order" as a "political calling" and not a quest for power.[61]

Before fundamentalists and evangelicals formed the religious right to "take back America," progressive evangelicals dreamed of "every Christian in America" understanding "God's will" and dedicating themselves to it.[62] John Perkins had a "great sense of urgency" in asking how to make "the country liveable for all people?"[63] Mark Hatfield longed for the "United States" to "decide to give leadership in combating global famine."[64] In 1978, Charles Fager, a *Sojourners* correspondent and delegate at the first National "No-Nukes" Strategy Conference at the University of Louisville, imagined a "second

---

59 Sabath, "Emily Post and Richard Nixon Revisited."
60 Ray Stedman and Charles Wagner, "Should the Church Be a Melting Pot?" *Christianity Today*, August 18, 1978; "Wagner . . . mentored some of the leading pastors of the seeker movement" including "Rick Warren, John Wimber, and Walt Kallestad." See Richard Kyle, *Evangelicalism: An Americanized Christianity* (Taylor & Francis, 2017), 234.
61 Clark Pinnock, "Charismatic Renewal for the Radical Church," *Sojourners*, February 1, 1975. https://sojo.net/magazine/february-1975/charismatic-renewal-radical-church.
62 MacDonald, "Prophetic Resistance."
63 John Perkins, "The Dividing Wall in America," *Sojourners*, February 1, 1976. https://sojo.net/magazine/february-1976/dividing-wall-america.
64 Mark Hatfield, "And Still They Hunger," *Sojourners*, January 1, 1975. https://sojo.net/magazine/january-1975/and-still-they-hunger.

American revolution" against nuclear power which would "change the course of American society." American evangelicals on the left saw themselves as members of both the United States and the kingdom of God.[65] In their thinking, though, it was necessary to conform the former to the latter.

Much like fundamentalists who crusaded for spiritual revival, young evangelicals found themselves in the "midst" of what Jim Wallis called, "a radical awakening."[66] Wallis believed that "spiritual renewal" would result in a "new political economy."[67] John Perkins described a "revival" that was "producing people who are less divided denominationally and theologically and are more open to the radical implications of the gospel than ever before."[68] The Christian World Liberation Front's charter issue of *Right On*, described the group's mission as the "New Berkeley Liberation Program." Their goal was to implement a "revolutionary program" in which "Jesus Christ" would "build" a "politically sound" movement which would establish "a liberated community" with "new forms of democratic participation." The CWLF wanted to "permanently challenge the present world system and act as a training center for the liberation of all people on this planet."

Terms like revival, renewal, awakening, and revolution described the process young progressive Christians believed could transform the United States and the world. While both fundamentalists and 1960s campus radicals shaped their understanding of social transformation, it was to nineteenth century revivalists that evangelicals on the left looked for historical justification and inspiration.

---

65 Robert Palmer, "Theology and Political Action," *Sojourners*, April 1, 1974. https://sojo.net/magazine/april-1974/theology-and-political-action.
66 Wallis, "Post-American Christianity."
67 Jim Wallis, "The Economy of Christian Fellowship," *Sojourners*, October 1, 1978. https://sojo.net/magazine/october-1978/economy-christian-fellowship.
68 Perkins, "Stoning the Prophets."

CHAPTER FOURTEEN

NORTHERN REVIVALISM IN THE 1970S

MAINSTREAM EVANGELICALS OFTEN PORTRAYED THEIR more progressive associates as "liberal" for harboring at best, a "left-of-center" position, or at worst, a "socio-economic philosophy approximat[ing] neo-Marxist economics."[1] Young evangelicals reinforced this narrative by publicly criticizing political conservatives. In 1976, Jim Wallis and Wes Granberg-Michaelson warned of plans to form an "alarming political initiative by the evangelical far right" which included Congressman John Conlan and Bill Bright, the founder of Campus Crusade for Christ. They were concerned that sincere Christians would naively involve themselves in "political purposes" for the furthering of an "idolatrous mingling of church and state."[2] Of course, this did not seem to be a problem when Senator Mark Hatfield and Jim Wallis partnered to further progressive political goals.

The evangelical left did not see themselves as guilty of their own criticisms since they believed their political agenda uniquely transcended earthly understandings and categories. Their brand of "biblical radicalism" rendered "old distinctions and disputes quite irrelevant," including common terms like

---

1 Turner, *Bill Bright and Campus Crusade for Christ*, 164; Edward Plowman, "Seeds of Schism: The Misery of Missouri," *Christianity Today*, May 10, 1974; "Evangelicals on Justice: Socially Speaking . . . " *Christianity Today*, December 21, 1973.
2 Jim Wallis, "Building Up the Commonlife," *Sojourners,* April 1, 1976. https://sojo.net/magazine/april-1976/building-commonlife.

"liberal" and "conservative."[3] Ron Sider "linked social justice to commitment to the authority of Scripture," not allegiance to a political party.[4] In a 1974 article entitled "Biblical Politics," Jim Wallis wrote that it was actually dangerous for Christians to "embrace a liberal political philosophy" because it could facilitate the "church becoming a power of the world" instead of the "kingdom of God."[5]

Convincing mainstream evangelicals that political ideas associated with the revolutionary New Left were, in fact, biblical, was a difficult task. If what progressives believed about social justice were true, it would mean that the most respected evangelical preachers and evangelists in recent memory had collectively erred in their understanding of basic truths like sin and the gospel. Such an incredible insinuation demanded something more than the authoritative claims of a handful of young activists and scholars. If progressives could demonstrate their ideas were legitimized by heroes within the American evangelical tradition, their argument would be more palpable. To accomplish this, they pointed to the Northern revivalists of the nineteenth century.

Preceding the modernist controversy, which solidified fundamentalists against the "social gospel" of theologically compromised mainline denominations, there existed an evangelical tradition which shared similarities with the radicals of the 1970s. Before what historian Timothy Smith called "the Great Reversal," in which theologically conservative Christians abandoned social action, mid-century preachers like "Edward Beecher, E. N. Kirk, Albert Barnes, George B. Cheever, [Charles] Finney and William Arthur" furrowed "the ground from which the social gospel sprang."[6] Timothy Smith's 1957 book, *Revivalism and Social Reform*, along with David Moberg's 1972 work *The Great*

3 Isaac Rottenberg, "A Skeptical Response to Social Concern," *Sojourners*, May 1, 1976. https://sojo.net/magazine/may-june-1976/skeptical-response-social-concern.
4 "Protestant Sects: 'The Body' Loses Its Earthly Head," *Christianity Today*, June 29, 1979.
5 Jim Wallis, "Biblical Politics," *Sojourners*, April 1, 1974. https://sojo.net/magazine/april-1974/biblical-politics.
6 Moberg, *The Great Reversal*, 30; Timothy Smith, *Revivalism and Social Reform: American Protestantism on the Eve of the Civil War*, (Wipf & Stock Publishers, 2004), 161.

Reversal, "helped evangelicals rediscover . . . a dimension of ministry largely abandoned during evangelicalism's fundamentalist phase."[7]

The Great Reversal followed on the heals of a string of "critical analysis of evangelicalism itself, by evangelicals" in the late sixties.[8] David Moberg, a sociologist from Marquette University and signer of the 1973 Chicago Declaration, argued for a reconciliation between "warring factions" who disagree "on the question of whether the gospel is personal or social."[9] Moberg believed the "revivalism of a century ago was clearly related to the fulfillment of Christian social responsibility."[10] This argument influenced fellow progressive evangelicals including Donald Dayton and his wife Lucille Sider Dayton.

In Donald Dayton's 1976 book, *Discovering an Evangelical Heritage,* much of which was compiled from a ten-part series published in the *Post-American,* Dayton shared discoveries concerning his own Wesleyan denomination, as well as the revivalist roots of other evangelical traditions. Dayton, who had chosen the values of the civil-rights movement over those of the evangelical culture he grew up in, was surprised to discover that his denomination itself "was a product of the closest parallel to the civil rights movement in American history—the abolitionist protest against slavery in the pre-Civil War period."[11] He lamented the fact that "movements whose egalitarian thrust once manifested itself in feminism and abolitionism [had] in more recent years moved back toward more traditional patterns of church life and social views."[12] Yet, he was optimistic about a "protest against the bourgeois church" similar to the "protest movements . . . of the nineteenth century, though . . . given different shape and character by the new context of the twentieth century."[13]

---

7 "Timothy Smith and the Recovery of the Nazarene Vision," *Holiness Today,* March 1999.
8 Carl Henry, "Decades of Gains and Losses," *Christianity Today,* March 12, 1976.
9 Moberg, *The Great Reversal,*12-13.
10 Ibid., 28.
11 Dayton, *Discovering an Evangelical Heritage,* 4.
12 Ibid., 140.
13 Ibid., 141.

Throughout the early part of the nineteenth century, the Christian character of New England changed drastically as both Unitarianism and Transcendentalism outpaced, and often replaced, Congregationalism. Both philosophies denied original sin and placed reason above revelation, thus producing an optimistic understanding of human and societal potential. These ideas, coupled with the Quakers and Shakers' concept of an "inner light," Wesleyan holiness, and Charles Finney's "decisional regeneration," created what historian Charles Singer calls the "New England Theology," which he states was "a mediating position holding to much of the Evangelical position while yielding at other points, particularly in regard to the doctrines of the atonement, divine sovereignty, and justification, in the direction of the Transcendentalist thought."[14]

Timothy Smith had understood the impact of humanist ideas on evangelicalism. He asserted in *Revivalism and Social Reform* that if "Thomas Paine, the free-thinking pamphleteer of the American and French revolutions" had "visited Broadway in 1865, he would have been amazed to find the nation conceived in rational liberty" and "at last fulfilling its democratic promise in the power of evangelical faith."[15] Smith devoted an entire chapter to "Evangelical Unitarianism," asserting that "evangelical doctrine dominated the Unitarian fold" and shared "Unitarianism's historical ethical, spiritual, and antisectarian concerns."[16] Unitarians and evangelicals had kindled "the first blaze of antislavery feeling" and evangelical abolitionists like Charles Finney and Theodore Weld owed a "debt to [William Lloyd] Garrison's *Liberator*."[17]

Progressive evangelicals, including David Moberg and Donald Dayton, either downplayed or ignored these unorthodox connections. Moberg did not address Unitarianism in *The Great Reversal* and Dayton complained that "most interpretations of the antislavery movement" emphasized "liberal and

---

14 Charles Singer, *A Theological Interpretation of American History*, International Library of Philosophy and Theology, (Craig Press, 1964), 65.
15 Smith, *Revivalism and Social Reform*, 7.
16 Ibid., 12.
17 Ibid., 180-181.

Unitarian aspects." Still, he decided to portray the dissident William Lloyd Garrison as "a product of revivalistic Evangelicalism" though Garrison believed "all reforms" including abolitionism, anti-capital punishment, and woman's rights, were "anti-Bible."[18] Dayton did, however, admit that Garrison was "somewhat erratic and anticlerical and often more of a liability."[19]

Both authors tried to paint revivalism's motivation for social reform as the logical consequence of orthodoxy. Neither fully reported the theological critiques many orthodox Christians made against the social reformers, especially from Southerners, other than to briefly mention Old School Presbyterian objections from theologians like Princeton Professor B.B. Warfield. Dayton depicted Princeton theology as a forerunner to fundamentalism which served to further emphasize the idea that the opponents of revivalism were one and the same with progressive evangelical's nemeses, the fundamentalists.[20]

Leaders of the evangelical left sensed an opportunity in attaching their cause to stalwarts like the great evangelist Charles Finney, whose image covered the front cover of Dayton's book. David Moberg said that *Discovering an Evangelical Heritage* deserved "to be read, reflected upon, and compared with present realities."[21] Richard Quebedeaux called it "A groundbreaking historical work" while Clark Pinnock said he learned "that evangelicalism has sources which led a century ago to radical social involvement and which could do so again."[22]

---

18 Dayton, *Discovering an Evangelical Heritage*, 26; Elizabeth Stanton, Susan Anthony, and Matilda Gage, *History of Woman Suffrage* (Susan B. Anthony, 1889), 382-383.
19 Dayton, *Discovering an Evangelical Heritage*, 26.
20 Dayton, *Discovering an Evangelical Heritage*, 26., 131; Historian Eugene Genovese writes that "at the very moment that northern churches were embracing theological liberalism and abandoning the Word for a Spirit of subjectivity, the southern churches were holding the line for Christian orthodoxy." See Eugene Genovese, *The Southern Front: History and Politics in the Cultural War* (University of Missouri Press, 1995), 12; For more on the Southern critique see Edward Crowther, *Southern Evangelicals and the Coming of the Civil War*, Studies in American Religion (E. Mellen Press, 2000) and Charles Singer, *A Theological Interpretation of American History*, International Library of Philosophy and Theology (Craig Press, 1964).
21 Dayton, *Discovering an Evangelical Heritage*, Back Cover.
22 Ibid.

It became common for evangelicals inspired by social justice to associate their movement with revivalism of the first half of the nineteenth century. Clark Pinnock thought the evangelical left should "go beyond scripture" in "fully implementing gospel principles" just as abolitionists did in applying "the Christian gospel" to the institution of slavery.[23] Jim Wallis recalled that he had "often said" that he was "a nineteenth-century American evangelical born in the wrong century."[24] Ron Sider later described his early years as a time when "younger evangelicals" returned to the "balanced position of much of 19th century evangelicalism" which embraced "justice while holding to central doctrines of the faith."[25] In 1977, Sider told a journalist that "during the nineteenth century the evangelist Charles Finney was also deeply involved in the anti-slavery movement. Unfortunately," he lamented, "we lost some of that concern in the early decades of this century."[26] Conservative evangelicals were not the only ones who pined for and sought to recover a forgotten but ideal period in American history. Young progressives found in revivalism a shared understanding of social sin, egalitarianism, and the importance of Christian political action in establishing the kingdom of God.

Dayton quoted Charles Finney as stating, "The Christian church was designed to make aggressive movements . . . to reform individuals, communities, and governments, and never rest until the kingdom . . . shall be given" to "the saints . . . until every form of iniquity shall be driven from the earth."[27] Such utopian dreams, brought about through immediate social action, characterized revivalism. Finney's theology posited that "God had given men and women a role in the shaping of society and that nothing had to be accepted

23 Clark Pinnock, "An Evangelical Theology of Human Liberation."
24 Jim Wallis, *The Great Awakening: Seven Ways to Change the World* (HarperCollins, 2009), 25.
25 Ron Sider, "History Shows Us Why Being Evangelical Matters," *Christianity Today*, November 21, 2016. https://www.christianitytoday.com/ct/2016/november-web-only/history-shows-us-why-being-evangelical-matters.html.
26 Williams, *The Weakness of Evangelical Ethics*, 3.
27 Dayton, *Discovering an Evangelical Heritage*, 21.

as it was."[28] He encouraged "women to pray and speak in . . . mixed assemblies," and called "for the use of church discipline on the social sin of 'slaveholding,'" which he believed to be a sin in and of itself.[29] In both Finney's and Dayton's minds, it was the "great business of the church . . . to reform the world."[30]

There was, however, something which could prohibit the realization of such goals. Finney believed that "revivals" were "hindered when ministers and churches take wrong ground in regard to any question involving human rights."[31] Dayton described the Wesleyans as practicing this common sentiment by testing "the spirituality of a church by its commitment to reform." Orange Scott, a leading Wesleyan preacher and abolitionist, even considered "all northern Christians, who neglect to lift up the warning voice and refuse to take sides with God's suffering poor," as "scarcely less guilty" than Southern slave-holders.[32]

This underlying assumption of corporate culpability and responsibility compelled many nineteenth century Northern evangelicals to get involved in new national organizations for social reform.[33] As a direct result of the ministries of Finney and other revivalists, "thousands . . . flocked to the Tract Society, the Sunday School Union, the temperance and peace organizations, and the Colonization Society."[34] The same impulse reflected itself in their theological descendants. Progressive evangelicals also engaged in activism motivated by a sense of group obligation.

For example, Jim Wallis called "Vietnam . . . a mirror in which our country could see itself."[35] Dale Brown thought Richard Nixon was only the "devil"

---

28 Ibid., 17.

29 Ibid., 21, 16.

30 Ibid., 21.

31 Ibid., 18.

32 Donald Dayton, "Recovering a Heritage - Part VI: Orange Scott and the Wesleyan Methodist," *Sojourners,* January 1, 1975, https://sojo.net/magazine/january-1975/recovering-heritage.

33 Dayton, *Discovering an Evangelical Heritage,* 77.

34 James Brewer Stewart, *Holy Warriors: The Abolitionists and American Slavery,* Rev. ed (New York: Hill and Wang, 1976), 35.

35 Wallis, *The New Radical,* 56.

if "we view him as having been our corporate personality reflective of the more glaring sins we commit together" such as, wasting money "in Southeast Asia," "imperialism in Chile," "unrepentant racism," and wanting peace with Russia for greedy reasons. A sense of shared national guilt haunted both movements and motivated its alleviation through social action and calling "the nation to repentance."[36]

It was common for the evangelical left to blame "individualism," as Moberg and Dayton did, for inaction against social evil.[37] However, both revivalists and progressives presupposed a form of individualism in order to promote social justice. Instead of working within the social framework of communities into which they were born, reform advocates attempted to destroy present social bonds and obligations while erecting new ones. These new social arrangements were achieved, not through natural alteration in community habit, but by individual consciences forcibly imposing their dictates. By extending the individual's guilt, responsibility, and action, even to regional matters outside their own tangible communities, reform-minded evangelicals individualized national sins. Their allegiance was not to a physical community, but rather to abstract principles existing in the mind of individuals. On this point Darryl Hart states, the evangelical left had an "almost utopian belief that with the right motives and arguments they could implement a more just society and a better form of government."[38]

For revivalists, the just society paralleled the kingdom of God. Jim Wallis sentimentally recounted that "nineteenth century evangelism resulted in so much social initiative" because "the meaning of the kingdom was kept in a central place."[39] Virginia Mollenkott sought to extend the logic of "18th and 19th century evangelicals who" believed the gospel would lead to a

---

36 Dale Brown, "'We Have Seen the Enemy . . . And They Is Us,'" *Sojourners*, April 1, 1975. https://sojo.net/magazine/april-1975/we-have-seen-enemyand-they-us.

37 Moberg, *The Great Reversal*, 90; Dayton, *Discovering an Evangelical Heritage*, 78.

38 Hart, *From Billy Graham to Sarah Palin*, 636.

39 Jim Wallis, "Interview: Carl Henry on Evangelical Identity," *Sojourners*, April 1, 1976, https://sojo.net/magazine/april-1976/interview-carl-henry-evangelical-identity.

racially "egalitarian society," by applying it to "male-female relationships" thus "de-absolutizing" the "sinful social order."[40] Donald Dayton told the story of Jonathan Blanchard, an abolitionist and founder of Wheaton College, who "came to Wheaton in 1860, still seeking 'a perfect state of society' and a college 'for Christ and his Kingdom.'"[41] Following in their footsteps, progressives sought to establish a "new community of those who seek to bear witness to the new order of the kingdom of God in the midst of the old order of the world."[42] No room existed for a theology that sanctioned "the social order the way it is."[43]

Both revivalists and progressive evangelicals criticized the political and social state of affairs in the worlds to which they belonged while dedicating themselves to projects of national reform. Carl Henry observed in a 1970 *Christianity Today* article that young evangelicals wanted "an honest look at many churches' idolatry of nationalism." At the same time, they also desired, aggressively promoting racial equality, greater involvement in "sociopolitical affairs," diminishing respect for authority figures who represented "economic power structures," the elevation of "young people" in controlling church policy, the elimination of "middle-class standards" of decency, and favoring the "underground church" over the "institutional church."[44] In short, young evangelicals wanted to change the hegemony of the nation they lived in.

In this desire, young evangelicals stood in an American protest tradition stemming from the nineteenth century. For example, Dayton wrote about Luther Lee, an abolitionist leader and founder of Wesleyan Methodism, who believed that slaves had the right to be free based upon "inalienable rights," language derived from the Declaration of Independence.[45] Over a century later,

---

40 Virginia Ramey Mollenkott, "Women and the Bible."
41 Dayton, *Discovering an Evangelical Heritage*, 11.
42 Wallis, "The New Community."
43 Wallis, "Interview: Carl Henry on Evangelical Identity."
44 Carl Henry, "Winds of Promise," *Christianity Today*, June 5, 1970.
45 Dayton, *Discovering an Evangelical Heritage*, 82.

John Perkins used similar logic when he wrote that Americans had "failed to implement" the Declaration's principles of "life, liberty, and happiness" as evidenced by the reality of "prejudice and oppression."[46] Many crusaders for social reform believed they were holding the nation accountable to its own ideals, which made their cause appear less revolutionary.

Though many New Left thinkers identified America's founding documents as innately unjust, another tradition believed they represented abstract propositions which had yet to be fully realized. In the "Gettysburg Address," Abraham Lincoln popularized the notion that liberty and equality were fundamental to the nation's identity, struggle, and perpetuity. Mark Hatfield greatly respected Lincoln and regularly paralleled his understanding of "national sins" with the concept of "corporate guilt" for things like racism, maldistribution, greed, waste, materialism, and nuclear buildup.[47] In a Senate speech "calling for a Day of Humiliation, Fasting and Prayer," Hatfield concluded by stating, "There is hope for a land and a people who have the capacity to recognize their sins and their faults, and turn from them."[48]

This national identity was not unique to politicians like Hatfield. Even Jim Wallis led protestors in singing songs like "The Star-Spangled Banner," "America the Beautiful," and "My Country, 'Tis of Thee," in his early days.[49] Wallis' patriotic sentiment seems to have diminished as he aged. In fact, the evangelical left, as a whole, saw "patriotism" as a dirty word. Yet, young evangelicals still kept a national focus. In a 1976 article about the nation's bicentennial, Wes Granberg-Michaelson stated that Scripture "unmasks the pretensions of our idols, ideologies, and nationalism. It de-Americanizes the gospel." However, he followed with the assertion: "The first task

---

46 John Perkins, "A Declaration Revisited," *Sojourners*, September 1, 1976, https://sojo.net/magazine/september-1976/declaration-revisited.

47 Eells and Nyberg, *Lonely Walk*, 24; Mark Hatfield, "The Prayer Breakfast," *Sojourners*, February 1, 1976, https://sojo.net/magazine/february-1976/prayer-breakfast; Mark Hatfield, "Repentance, Politics, and Power," *Sojourners*, January 1, 1974, https://sojo.net/magazine/january-1974/repentance-politics-and-power.

48 Mark Hatfield, *Between a Rock and a Hard Place*, (Pocket Books, 1977), 105.

49 Wallis, *Revive Us Again*, 55.

of Christians is to reveal the truth about America rather than celebrate its dreams."[50] Even in their criticism, progressive evangelicals echoed their revivalist heritage by taking responsibility for the nation as a whole. It was also to nineteenth century revivalists that they looked for inspiration as they worked toward reform.

One of Donald Dayton's detailed examples of nineteenth century reform concerned the events at Oberlin College in Ohio, which he described as "a product of the revivalism of evangelist Charles G. Finney." The school started in the 1830s as an outgrowth of Lane Seminary, which, under the leadership of Lyman Beecher, held to a "brand of reform" which "was more moderate and 'polite,'" including "'gradual' abolitionism and colonization" on the slavery question. However, Theodore Weld, a student at Lane and former assistant to Charles Finney, successfully convinced the members of the campus colonization society to instead form a society for the promotion of "immediate abolitionism."[51]

Fearing that abolitionism would detract from the school's mission of preparing preachers of the gospel, Oberlin's trustee board forbade discussing slavery and fired a professor who was on the student's side. In reaction, forty students left the school and joined the The Oberlin Institute, a colony and school influenced by Charles Finney, which valued a "'communitarian' and 'lifestyle' oriented radicalism." The Institute's code of conduct even undermined the concept of private property by stating that students were to consider their individual estates as belonging to "a community of property."[52]

The existing parallels between the campus protests of the 1960s and the situation at Oberlin were unmistakable. Oberlin's goal was to make "the whole Christian Church in effect an 'anti-slavery society.'" The Oberlin

---

50 Wes Granberg-Michaelson, "No King But Caesar."
51 Donald Dayton, "Recovering a Heritage- Part III: The Lane Rebellion and the Founding of Oberlin College," *Sojourners*, October 1, 1974, https://sojo.net/magazine/october-1974/recovering-heritage.
52 Ibid.

Church even passed a resolution which stated, "as Slavery is a Sin no person shall be invited to preach or Minister to this church, or any Br. be invited to commune who is a slaveholder." The Oberlin Anti-Slavery Society worked "for the 'immediate emancipation of the whole colored race,'" and "Oberlin provided at least sixteen of the famous 'Seventy' sent out as agents of the American Anti-Slavery Society." The "peace movement also found support at Oberlin" in the Oberlin Non-Resistance Society and the Oberlin Peace Society. The school endorsed "progressive education," "civil disobedience," the concept of a "Higher" or "Divine Law," and students "were for the most part vegetarian," "sympathize[d] with John Brown," and defended "the Northern cause during the Civil War." The local district attorney saw "the Oberlinites as revolutionaries" and thought they should "preach 'the Bible and not politics.'"[53] Young evangelicals felt they could relate to the revivalists at Oberlin since they experienced similar reactions for their behavior.

The evangelical left also admired revivalists for successfully making churches and Christian institutions vehicles for social reform. From the pages of *Right On*, Mark Hatfield encouraged:

> Let us recall that the church of Jesus Christ was the reforming influence of the 18th and 19th centuries: child labor, abolition of slavery, caring for the needy. Let us not abdicate this work to agencies which do not have the underpinning of love and motivation of Jesus Christ. The churches, the Christian communities again can act and not merely adopt statements and resolutions.[54]

Similarly, Donald and Lucille Sider Dayton also highlighted the 1848 Seneca Falls meeting in New York, which jump started the woman's rights

---

53 Donald Dayton, "Recovering a Heritage- Part V: The Rescue Case," *Sojourners*, December 1, 1974, https://sojo.net/magazine/december-1974/recovering-heritage; Donald Dayton, "Recovering a Heritage- Part IV: The 'Christian Radicalism' of Oberlin College," *Sojourners*, November 1, 1974, https://sojo.net/magazine/november-1974/recovering-heritage.
54 Mark Hatfield, "Mark Hatfield on World Hunger," *Right On*, March 1975.

movement, because it took place in a Wesleyan Church.[55] The church's new political function required direct action, not merely equipping members who were statesmen with biblical governing principles.

Therefore, reform minded evangelicals thought it imperative to convert all Christian institutions to the reform agenda in order to accomplish the goal of societal transformation. An example of this can be seen at Campus Crusade's Explo '72 conference when the People's Christian Coalition and a group sent by the Mennonite Central Committee protested the war in Vietnam. They handed out literature and sported signs and banners with phrases like, "Choose this day—make disciples or make bombs, love your enemies or kill your enemies," or, "'Cross or Flag' and 'Christ or Country.'" When the "messengers of peace" disrupted a Flag ceremony by chanting, "Stop the war! Stop the war! Stop the war!" police had to respond.[56]

In reaction to their dismissal, the protestors issued a statement in which they cited "love for fellowmen" and "ultimate allegiance . . . to Christ" as their motivation for opposing "immoral American involvement in Indochina." The statement maintained that it was not "by might nor by power but by the Lord's Spirit that we are saved from any principalities and powers of evil in our world." The protestors believed that the evangelical church's "misplaced allegiance" had made them silently complicit and caused them to identify "Jesus Christ with the military." Though their New Left inclinations caused them to detest "americanized civil religion," they were, in effect, engaging in it by thinking of themselves as a prophetic witness to both the church and the nation.[57] They believed both unbelievers and Christians alike were in need of conversion. This conclusion was not far removed from the way many Christians involved in Northern social crusades thought in the nineteenth century.

---

55 Donald Dayton and Lucille Sider Dayton, "Recovering a Heritage, Part II: Evangelical Feminism, by Donald W. Dayton and Lucille Sider Dayton," *Sojourners,* August 1, 1974, https://sojo.net/magazine/august-september-1974/recovering-heritage.
56 Peter Ediger, "Explo '72," *Sojourners,* September 1, 1972. https://sojo.net/magazine/fall-1972/explo-72.
57 Ibid.

In 1972, *Right On* quoted the famous nineteenth century abolitionist Frederick Douglas' indictment against the church of his day. According to Douglas, the "Christianity of this land and the Christianity of Christ" were separated by "the widest possible difference." One was "good, pure, and holy," while the other, "bad, corrupt, and wicked." The "Christianity of Christ" stood in diametric opposition to "the corrupt, slave-holding, women-whipping, cradle-plundering, partial, and hypocritical Christianity" which characterized the United States. The editors at the Christian World Liberation Front believed Douglas stood as an inspiration for them since "the evils against which he fought have been replaced by others no less vicious." For young progressives, the "true marks of the Christian" were found in actions similar to Douglas'.[58]

Both revivalists and progressive evangelicals believed in the existence of a "higher law" found in a more complete gospel and exemplified by the life of Christ. Donald Dayton recounted the words of Henry Peck, a Mental and Moral Philosophy Professor at Oberlin, who believed the "'Divine Will was well expounded in the life of Christ' whose gospel was such that 'those who should follow Him, should minister good to the needy . . . and that it would strike the iron from countless wretches unjustly bound.'"[59] Northern anti-slavery missionaries answered the call to preach the whole gospel where it was not followed. Dayton wrote about Adam Crooks, a Wesleyan missionary who went to North Carolina describing his goal as pronouncing "that Gospel which proclaims liberty to the captives, and the opening of the prisons to them that are bound." Another figure Dayton quoted was Luther Lee, a Wesleyan minister who left the

---

58 "A Word from Frederick Douglas," *Right On*, March 1972.
59 Dayton, "Recovering a Heritage- Part III: The Lane Rebellion and the Founding of Oberlin College"; Historian Stanley Harrold notes: "From the 1830s onward, abolitionists denounced what they called a proslavery gospel that either ignored the issue of slavery or actively denied that Christian principles favored emancipation. In contrast, they preached what they called a 'whole,' 'pure,' or 'free,' gospel, emphasizing Bible precepts that non-abolitionists avoided." See Stanley Harrold, *The Abolitionists and the South*, 1831-1861 (University Press of Kentucky, 2015), 92-93.

Methodist Episcopal Church over its unwillingness to support immediate emancipation. Lee believed the gospel was "so radically reformatory, that to preach it fully and clearly, is to attack and condemn all wrong, and to assert and defend all righteousness."[60] These early articulations of a social gospel centered more around man's ability to transform society than they did Christ's ability to transform man.

Embedded into the fabric of this gospel were egalitarian assumptions and, to some extent, approval for the use of radical measures in achieving them. Dayton wrote about Luther Lee's sermon entitled "Dying to the Glory of God," which was a response to the execution of John Brown after Brown's failure to lead a violent slave revolt. The sermon argued, based on the Bible and the American Revolution, that it was sometimes right to "oppose oppression, and defend human liberty . . . by force of arms.'"[61] Dayton recounted two individuals affiliated with Oberlin who died as a result of assisting Brown. One professor at the college referred to them as "martyrs for liberty." A board of trustees member called Brown "one of the Wise Men of our times." A toast was also made for Brown at "a joint meeting of the men's literary societies" which hailed him as the "hero of Harper's Ferry—the true representative of the American idea!"[62] Though the kinds of "radical" measures progressive evangelicals advocated were non-violent, a hint of the same revolutionary spirit continued in them. Over a century later and on the other side of the country, Sharon Gallagher of the Christian World Liberation Front opined, "I would say with" Julia Ward Howe, "As he died to make [people] holy, let us die to make [people] free."[63]

The kind of freedom Sharon Gallagher proposed, as evidenced by her altering the Battle Hymn to read "people," instead of "men," included more

60 Donald Dayton, "Recovering a Heritage- Part VII: The Sermons of Luther Lee," *Sojourners*, February 1, 1975, https://sojo.net/magazine/february-1975/recovering-heritage.
61 Dayton, *Discovering an Evangelical Heritage*, 83.
62 Dayton, *Discovering an Evangelical Heritage*, 61-62.
63 Sharon Gallagher, "Ode to Caesar," *Sojourners*, March 1, 1976, https://sojo.net/magazine/march-1976/ode-caesar.

than the destruction of a slave labor system. She, like many progressive evangelicals and revivalists wanted to challenge traditional gender roles. Regarding her personal journey into feminism, Gallagher wrote: "Other allies I discovered were the suffragettes of the last century. In their writings I saw women who based their ideas of liberty and equality firmly on the Bible and on who they were before God: they, too, were made 'in his image.'" Significantly, she added: "Their writings gave me confidence that I wasn't simply doing a twentieth-century gloss on the Bible's stance on women."[64]

Dayton observed that "feminism arose naturally in the context of abolitionism."[65] Letha Scanzoni agreed stating, "The women's rights movement is nothing new. It is a resurgence of the drive for equal rights that was sparked in the last century by women who were active in the abolitionist cause."[66] Luther Lee and "Methodist crusader" Francis Willard each supported the ordination of women.[67] Theodore Weld influenced Charles Finney to encourage "women to speak and pray in . . . mixed meetings."[68] Benjamin Roberts, a founder of the Free Methodist Church, advocated "an egalitarian marriage relationship."[69] Many revivalists sounded very similar to feminist evangelicals.

Both Donald and Lucille Sider Dayton worked to influence evangelicals toward an egalitarian ethic by utilizing these nineteenth century examples. They submitted a paper on the topic to both the 1974 Annual Convention of the Christian Holiness Association and the 1974 Chicago Workshop, which was a follow up to the meeting which crafted the Chicago Declaration.[70] The paper's title was, "Women in the Holiness Movement."

---

64 Virginia Hearn, *Our Struggle to Serve*, 96.
65 Dayton, *Discovering an Evangelical Heritage*, 61-62.
66 Letha Scanzoni, "The Feminists and the Bible," *Christianity Today*, February 2, 1973.
67 Dayton, "Recovering a Heritage- Part VII: The Sermons of Luther Lee;" Dayton, *Discovering an Evangelical Heritage*, 95.
68 Dayton, *Discovering an Evangelical Heritage*, 87.
69 Ibid., 92.
70 Donald Dayton and Lucille Sider Dayton, "Women in the Holiness Movement," May 1, 1974, Title Page.

In addition to Lee, Weld, Roberts, and Willard, the Daytons included examples of Christian women who exceeded traditional boundaries like Susanna Wesley, the wife of John Wesley, evangelist Phoebe Palmer, and Catherine Booth, the wife of William Booth who founded the Salvation Army. There was no mistaking their argument. A Christian influenced practice of challenging traditional gender rolls "continued well into the 20th century" but had "declined in recent years."[71] By harkening back to the heroes of the previous century, progressive evangelicals thought they may be able to convince the broader evangelical world to accept their egalitarian understanding.

Interestingly, evangelical progressives did not focus on other revivalist efforts to change society such as the Sunday School, Temperance, and Anti-Masonic movements. Nor, did they highlight revivalism's social rules when it came to dress and dancing. Some of these features became part of the peculiarities of fundamentalism, but young evangelicals rejected them. Instead, the evangelical left gleaned from Northern revivalism a justification for their understanding of social sin and the necessity for immediate political response in order to usher in a more egalitarian kingdom of God. They saw their fight for racial, gender, and class equality as a continuation of the nineteenth century abolitionism, feminism, and communal living. Just as revivalists transformed Northern Christianity by focusing on both personal piety and social reform, progressive evangelicals tried to change the nature of American evangelicalism. In a certain sense, "His truth" was still "marching on" from the pages of 1970s young evangelical publications like the *Post-American, The Other Side,* and *Right On.*

---

71 Ibid., 23.

PART FOUR

THE FALL AND RISE OF THE EVANGELICAL LEFT

THOUGH SOME STUDENTS OF HISTORY have started analyzing the early years of the evangelical left, little study is done on their connection to the current social justice movement within mainstream evangelicalism. Yet, a strong connection does exist. In a very significant sense, the pioneers of progressive evangelicalism are currently enjoying the fruits of their labor. Because the media often associates the term "evangelical" with Republican politics, the story of how progressive evangelicals from the 1970s gained influence within mainstream evangelicalism almost a half century later is often ignored. Perhaps, this is the most important part of their story, though, because it is the climax. Before the dawn of success, young evangelicals drank the cup of defeat, only to reemerge as powerful force in national politics.

CHAPTER FIFTEEN

THE FALL

AS THE DECADE OF THE 1970s progressed, members of the evangelical left sensed their movement was ascending. Jim Wallis anticipated that "the decline of the New Left" would open the door for Christian "prophetic witness and social justice."[1] At Fuller Theological Seminary and Wheaton College, a new generation of professors were ascending, many of whom were influenced by New Left ideas. At some evangelical colleges, an urban focus which emphasized social concern took root. The existence of organizations like the "Urban Life Center in Chicago, Westmont College's San Francisco program, and Messiah College's inner-city campus in North Philadelphia" showed a new interest in urban communities.[2]

The attitudes of individual students were changing as well. In the 1950s, three quarters of Fuller students believed evangelism was more important than social justice. By the 1970s, only around half the students felt the same way.[3] Senator Mark Hatfield's 1970 commencement speech at the seminary sparked a slew of anti-Vietnam War protests from students and faculty. In the balcony, students displayed a banner stating, "We're with you, Mark" as the senator encouraged Fuller to provide an alternative to the "Biblical Nationalists" on war, race, and wealth distribution in order to encapsulate the "entirety of the gospel."[4]

1 Sider, *The Chicago Declaration*, 142.
2 Ibid., 14.
3 Marsden, *Reforming Fundamentalism*, 254.
4 Mark Hatfield, *Conflict and Conscience.* Waco, TX: (Word Incorporated, 1971), 20, 24, 25.

A growing contingent of progressive students also emerged at Wheaton. Around fifty students protested Barry Goldwater during a 1964 speech on Wheaton's campus due to his state's rights position on integration. In the late 1960s, anti-war groups formed on campus such as "Students Concerned about Vietnam" and "Americans for Democratic Action." Students gave Senator Mark Hatfield a standing ovation after his anti-war speech in 1970. Two years later, George McGovern spoke to an overflow crowd touting his Christian credentials by quoting from John Winthrop's "City Upon a Hill" speech.[5] Though Wheaton was still fairly politically conservative, things were changing.

Ron Sider optimistically observed that evangelicals were "beginning to transcend the unholy dichotomy of evangelism or social concern."[6] In 1974, Richard Quebedeaux described young evangelicals as interested in "action in the world," "the proclamation of the Gospel in its entirely," "discipleship," and a church that functioned "corporately not only as the community of the saved but also as an instrument of reconciliation."[7]

Unfortunately, for those invested in the movement, a number of factors converged halfway through the decade which suspended the momentum progressive evangelicals felt coming off the Chicago Declaration and the Lausanne Covenant. First, identity politics fractured the movement. Even during the first 1973 workshop in Chicago, Sider recorded that "the black participants sharply attacked the planning committee for including only one black in the decision-making process" and rejected "the proposed statement on racism" offering their own alternative. Nancy Hardesty also "urged the largely male gathering to take the issue of women's rights seriously and include more than the one word on sexism in the proposed draft." John Howard Yoder complained: "Blacks have a paragraph they can redo; women have a word they can redo; but there is nothing at all about war."[8]

---

5 Swartz, "The Evangelical Left and the Politicization of Evangelicalism," 277-278, 282.
6 Sider, *The Chicago Declaration*, 13.
7 Quebedeaux, *The Young Evangelicals*, 74.
8 Sider, *The Chicago Declaration*, 26-27.

These same forces haunted the movement until its fragmentation. In the spring of 1974, a conclave sponsored by Calvin college's political science department met to discuss social action along with many participants who were present at the 1973 Thanksgiving Workshop in Chicago. The president of the National Black Evangelical Association, William Bentley, ridiculed the conference for being a "predominantly white male audience" while "some female participants" criticized "the absence of a platform representative for the women's issue."[9]

Later in the year, the second Thanksgiving Workshop divided, in part, over radical proposals. John Alexander introduced "an economic-life-styles proposal calling on Christians to try to live on $2,000 a year." The "woman's caucus" wanted to examine "Bible translations and Christian-education materials for use of 'sexist language.'" The creation of "six separate task forces . . . seemed fragmented to many participants." One attendee, history professor Richard Pierard, observed, "Last year's meeting was focused; we wrote the declaration. This year everyone was doing his or her own thing."[10]

By the third Thanksgiving Workshop in 1975, *Christianity Today* reported some participates "gloomily predicted the group's demise." William Bentley "lashed out at the group for being too white-minded" and Jim Wallis, along with others said they planned to drop out of Evangelicals for Social Action which organized the workshops. However, by this time, Evangelicals for Social Action and Sojourners were joined by the Evangelical Women's Caucus, with "over a dozen regional chapters," the Black Evangelical Association, and the Association for Public Justice which all helped divide and channel various progressive evangelical causes.[11]

This ideological narrowness made it hard for the evangelical left to appeal to the working class demographic which eventually composed the populist

---

9 Edward Plowman, "Seeds of Schism: The Misery of Missouri," *Christianity Today*, May 10, 1974.
10 Edward Plowman, "Carrying the Cross in the U.S.S.R.," *Christianity Today*, December 20, 1974.
11 Swartz, "The Evangelical Left and the Politicization of Evangelicalism," 284.

religious right. David Swartz reports, "well over two-thirds of the evangelical left held education, social service, and religious jobs . . . 85 percent of *Reformed Journal* readers [where Richard Mouw contributed] and 86 percent of *Sojourners* readers held a college degree. The median educational level of *The Other Side* readers was two years of graduate work."[12] These and other outlets did not feature articles on raising children or other practical concerns. The impact of this lack of emphasis became more evident as communes ended when members got married and had children.[13]

In addition, the political and moral issues impacting evangelicals in local communities, such as school prayer, abortion, homosexual adoption, equal protection, and religious tax exemption, were relatively ignored by progressive evangelical publications. Instead, their social issues tended to focus on the application of broad and abstract principles to national or international relationships—content not as relatable to those outside the "knowledge class."

Wes Granberg-Michaelson described well this demographic. He observed that "in seminaries and social action bureaucracies of the church in the United States, it [was] becoming acceptable and almost chic to confide to others that you are a Marxist."[14] Though Granberg-Michaelson did not think it ideal, he could well have described his own life when he observed that "many young ministers . . . reacted against the protective piety of conservative Christianity" to see "their role as prophets of social justice." This tendency inclined trained pastors away from local church ministry and instead toward working for their denomination or becoming "social workers, organizers, or even politicians."[15]

In contrast to the 1980s "religious right," hardly any leaders of the evangelical left were pastors, let alone televangelists with working class audiences. In general, they were skeptical of technology and relied primarily on print

---

12 Swartz, *Moral Minority*, 149.
13 Eskridge, *God's Forever Family*, 255.
14 Wes Granberg-Michaelson, "Liberating the Church."
15 Wes Granberg-Michaelson, "Politics and Spirituality," *Sojourners*, April 1, 1974, https:// sojo.net/magazine/april-1974/politics-and-spirituality.

media to disseminate their message. Many progressive evangelicals feared technology for its dehumanizing tendency and the fact that it was controlled by corporations or the government. They frequently used the term "technocracy" to represent the entangling web of modern technology and the power over individuals and social groups it represented.[16] Perhaps as a partial result, they were largely left out of news stories explaining popular evangelical and media driven social developments in 1976 surrounding what *Time Magazine* called the "Year of the Evangelical."

Initially, Southern Baptist and "born again" President Jimmy Carter's election in 1976 appeared to be a possible opportunity for the formation of a more politically progressive Christianity. But, those dreams quickly evaporated. Instead, the contrast between politically conservative and progressive evangelicals became especially sharp after the failure of President Carter to win reelection in 1980. This ended up helping the larger conservative contingent, though Christians on both sides of the political spectrum disapproved of many of the president's positions.

Conservatives thought Carter was weak on national defense and the economy. More importantly, his support for the Equal Right's Amendment and denying tax-exempt status to Christian schools, along with his approval for a measure of homosexual normalization and abortion sealed his fate with most politically conservative evangelicals.[17] In 1976, fifty-six percent of "white Baptists" voted for Carter. By 1980, only thirty-four percent did.[18]

Progressive evangelicals were likewise disappointed by Carter's "failing to follow through in his human rights rhetoric; for increasing defense spending; for a passive approach to the energy crisis; for not lobbying hard enough

16 "Technocracy and Women's Liberation," *Sojourners*, June 1, 1972, https://sojo.net/magazine/summer-1972/technocracy-and-womens-liberation; William Stringfellow, "Technocracy and the Human Witness," *Sojourners*, November 1, 1976, https://sojo.net/magazine/november-1976/technocracy-and-human-witness; Jim Wallis, "A Conversation with Young Evangelicals."

17 Fitzgerald, *The Evangelicals*, 304, 311.

18 Sara Diamond, *Right-Wing Movements in the United States, 1945-1992* (University of California, Berkeley, 1993), 362.

to pass the Equal Rights Amendment; for inadequate educational funding; for increasing the nuclear threat; for failing to help the poor; and for elevating efficiency above compassion."[19] Unfortunately for Christian progressives, even if they wanted to capitalize on the emotional disappointment many evangelicals felt in Jimmy Carter's presidency, they lacked the platform to do it. They simply could not compete for popular audiences with the politically conservative evangelical personalities who emerged in the late 1970s and early 1980s on television and radio stations. As figures like Jerry Falwell and Pat Robertson stole headlines, the evangelical left remained on the periphery in academia and smaller activist groups. The movement was fracturing.

Some progressive evangelicals focused on more reachable goals. Wes Granberg-Michaelson, for example, left politics and worked to address issues like climate change in the World Council of Churches and to further ecumenicism in the Reformed Church of America. Other leaders like Sharon Gallagher, Samuel Escobar, and John Howard Yoder became more influential in cultural, educational, and political circles, respectively, but were not very influential in mainstream evangelicalism.[20] Still, others left the movement altogether. John Alexander became disillusioned with the evangelical left in the mid 1980s. He stated that progressive Christians' obsession with rights violations was "boring and had a stunningly different tenor from Jesus' teaching." In his mind, "they were no better than schismatic fundamentalists at getting along with folks, and often their sexual stance was roughly as destructive as nuclear war."[21]

Despite the demise of progressive evangelicalism, groups like Sojourners, Evangelicals for Social Action, and *The Other Side* remained active. Unfortunately for them, mainstream evangelicals did not join their movement. As a result, *Sojourners* and *The Other Side* became more ecumenical, partnering with "Quaker, Catholic, and leftist" participants. This in turn

---

19 Swartz, *Moral Minority*, loc 3920.
20 Nation, *John Howard Yoder*; Swartz, *Moral Minority*, 258.
21 Alexander, *Being Church*, loc 63.

helped alienate mainstream evangelicals even more throughout the 1980s since most evangelicals resisted partnering with what they considered to be other religions.[22]

However, the advance of secularism and the more ecumenical aspects of the Pro-Life movement started breaking down evangelical suspicion of outside groups. Alienation toward the evangelical left started to evaporate in the 2000s as a new generation of Christian leaders, influenced by progressive ideas, started new ministries and gained leadership positions in established evangelical organizations. Remarkably, members of the evangelical left like Ron Sider, Richard Mouw, John Perkins, and Jim Wallis gained a measure of acceptance within mainstream evangelicalism forty years after they signed the Chicago Declaration.

---

22 Swartz, *Moral Minority*, 249; Gasaway, *Progressive Evangelicals and the Pursuit of Social Justice*, 15-16.

CHAPTER SIXTEEN

THE RISE

IN 1981, RON SIDER HAD high hopes of achieving "a fairly broadly based centrist movement led by prominent leaders of established evangelical agencies."[1] Throughout the 1980s and 90s Sider championed a comprehensive pro-life position through Evangelicals for Social Action, the American Coalition for Life, and Call to Renewal, speaking on the topic everywhere from Christian universities to the steps of the White House.[2] Sider's pro-life views were published in his 1987 book, *Completely Pro-Life: Building a Consistent Stance on Abortion, the Family, Nuclear Weapons, The Poor.* Yet, in 2019, he lamented, "Sometimes I feel like I've worked very hard in the evangelical community and I haven't succeeded very well."[3]

However, Ron Sider ultimately influenced a new crop of both progressive and conservative evangelicals. David Gushee, a prominent progressive ethics professor at Mercer University, worked under Sider in the early 1990s.[4] Gushee states, "I liked and identified with what I saw in him," and credits Sider with being his "guide into the 'card-carrying' evangelical world."[5] To

---

1 Ron Sider, "What Should Be the Shape of the Evangelical Political Involvement in the 80's?," March 20, 1981, Folder "1981," ESA Archives.
2 Sider was notably the keynote at Sojourners "Peace Pentecost" in 1985.
3 Russell Moore, "A Conversation with Ronald J. Sider," August 21, 2019, 18:40.
4 David Gushee. "David P. Gushee." Accessed March 12, 2020. http://www.davidpgushee. com/davidpgushee.
5 David Gushee, "Interview with David P. Gushee, author of Still Christian: Following Jesus Out of American Evangelicalism," *Reading Religion*, Accessed March 12, 2020. http://readingreligion.org/content/interview-david-p-gushee-author-still-christian-following-jesus-out-american-evangelicalism.

Gushee, who announced his departure from American evangelicalism in 2017, Sider's political ideas represented "a mature, balanced, well-informed, richly biblical Christian political ethic."[6]

Ron Sider's impact can also be seen today in more conservative organizations like the Ethics and Religious Liberty Commission (ERLC) for the Southern Baptist Convention, whose purpose is to engage "the culture with the gospel" and promote "religious liberty and human flourishing."[7] In 2016, the ERLC produced a number of resources which Sider contributed to, including three stand alone short videos, a conference lecture, and a roundtable discussion.

In "Why is it Important for Pastors to Help Their Churches Adopt a Whole-Life/Pro-Life Worldview?" Sider argued, "it's crucial to understand that pro-life leads to a concern for a whole bunch of issues."[8] In a speech entitled, "Across the Spectrum: Why Abortion is a Social Justice Issue for All Evangelicals," Sider criticized the pro-life movement for inconsistency in failing to care about "poverty and starvation and smoking and environmental degradation and racism and capital punishment." In a closing remark Sider added, "I think there's probably nothing that white evangelicals could do to persuade more African American Christians to join the pro-life movement against abortion than for us to say that precisely because we are consistently pro-life we join them in insisting that black lives matter." The comment received an ovation from the ERLC audience.[9]

In 2019, Russell Moore, the president of the ERLC since 2013, called Sider "gutsy" and someone whom he agreed with "on a lot of things" and wanted

6 Ron Sider, Scandal of Evangelical Politics, The: Why Are Christians Missing the Chance to Really Change the World? (Baker Publishing Group, 2008), Back Cover.

7 The Ethics & Religious Liberty Commission of the Southern Baptist Convention, "ERLC: About," Accessed March 11, 2020. https://erlc.com/about.

8 Ron Sider, Why Is It Important for Pastors to Help Their Churches Adopt a Whole-Life/pro-Life Worldview?, The Ethics and Religious Liberty Commission of the Southern Baptist Convention, 2016, https://erlc.com/resource-library/video-explainers/why-is-it-important-for-pastors-to-help-their-churches-adopt-a-whole-life-pro-life-worldview.

9 Ron Sider, "Across the Spectrum: Why Abortion Is a Social Justice Issue for All Evangelicals," The Ethics and Religious Liberty Commission of the Southern Baptist Convention, 2016. 6:00, 13:00, https://erlc.com/resource-library/event-messages/across-the-spectrum-why-abortion-is-a-social-justice-issue-for-all-evangelicals.

to "learn from" in regard to faithfulness. Though the two did not agree on the subject of capital punishment, Moore stated, "I really have benefitted a lot from his writing over the years" and "I am very much appreciative of the courage [he has] demonstrated in trying to follow Jesus." Moore revealed that he personally owned "two shelves" of Sider's books.[10]

Leading up to the 2016 election, *Christianity Today* published Ron Sider's article, "Why I Am Voting for Hillary Clinton." In it, Sider argued that Democratic candidate Hillary Clinton had "a decades-long history of working hard for racial and economic justice" while Republican candidate Donald Trump's "recent pro-life stand" wasn't credible, his "marriage record [was] horrendous," and his "call to ban all Muslims from immigrating to the United States" violated "religious freedom." Sider's "completely pro-life agenda," which had previously inspired him to oppose President Obama's "insurance coverage for contraceptives" proposal, now guided him to reject President Trump, a decision notably supported by a mainstream neo-evangelical publication.[11]

In 2020, Sider again opposed Donald Trump by publishing *The Spiritual Danger of Donald Trump: 30 Evangelical Christians on Justice, Truth, and Moral Integrity*. He described it as "a book to call people to think biblically about this election and about the character of candidates."[12] Other contributors to the work included Mark Galli, the former editor and chief of *Christianity Today*, and Samuel Escobar.

Sider's ideas on social justice left their mark on evangelical leaders such as John Piper of *Desiring God*, Jonathan Leeman of 9 Marks ministries, John Fea from Messiah College, as well as a younger generation of evangelicals like media contributor Jonathan Merritt, author Jemar Tisby, provost of the Southern Baptist Theological Seminary, Matthew Hall, and popular Southern

---

10 "A Conversation with Ronald J. Sider," 00:15, 0:55, 1:49, 4:05, 5:09, 5:15, https://www. russellmoore.com/2019/08/21/a-conversation-with-ronald-j-sider.

11 Steensland and Goff, *The New Evangelical Social Engagement*, 215; Ron Sider, "Ron Sider: Why I Am Voting for Hillary Clinton," *Christianity Today*, October 2016.

12 Samuel Smith, "'The Spiritual Danger of Trump:' New Book Asks Evangelicals to Rethink Their Vote in 2020," accessed July 13, 2020, https://www.christianpost.com/news/the-spiritual-danger-of-trump-new-book-asks-evangelicals-to-rethink-their-vote-in-2020.html.

Baptist pastor David Platt.[13] Today, Ron Sider enjoys more mainstream evangelical acceptance than perhaps any of the original 1970s era progressive evangelical thinkers with the exception of Richard Mouw.

Richard Mouw's influence on modern evangelicalism cannot be underestimated. He served both as the president of Fuller Seminary (1993-2013) and the Association of Theological Schools and continues to speak at places like Dordt University, Pepperdine University, Southern Seminary, Wheaton College, and Northeastern University. Mouw's writings are featured on Biologos, where he also serves on the board of directors, The Gospel Coalition, *In All Things, First Things,* and *Christianity Today.* He has also contributed to think tanks influential in many evangelical seminaries such as the Oikonomia Network and the Acton Institute. Mouw received a Lifetime Achievement Award from Christians for Biblical Equality, whose mission is "to eliminate the power imbalance between men and women resulting from theological patriarchy," as well as The Abraham Kuyper Prize for Excellence in Reformed Theology and Public Life from Princeton Theological Seminary.[14]

13 John Piper, "World Hunger and Us," *Desiring God,* November 1, 1981, https://www.desiring-god.org/messages/world-hunger-and-us; Jonathan Leeman, "Week #10—What Christians Should Ask of Government: To Treat People Equally (Justice and Identity Politics)," *9 Marks,* November 3, 2016, https://www.9marks.org/article/week-10-what-christians-should-ask-of-government-to-treat-people-equally-justice-and-identity-politics/#_ftnref2; John Fea, "Ron Sider: I'm Still an 'Evangelical,'" *The Way of Improvement Leads Home* (blog), January 17, 2020, https://thewayofimprovement.com/2020/01/17/ron-sider-im-still-an-evangelical/; Jonathan Merritt [@JonathanMerritt], 2019, "In 2008, I read a book that shattered many of my assumptions about God, faith, and what it means to follow Jesus. It was called 'Rich Christians in an Age of Hunger' by Ron Sider," Twitter, April 30, 2019, 11:24 p.m., https://twitter.com/JonathanMerritt/status/1123246756257587201; Jemar Tisby [@JemarTisby], 2018, "While it is tempting to create new declarations . . . never overlook the saints of the past who have already done this work . . . To address contemporary debates, sometimes it is not necessary to re-litigate but simply to re-discover," Twitter, September 10, 2018, 5:39 p.m., https://twitter.com/JemarTisby/status/1039267078447001607; Matthew Hall [@MatthewJHall], 2016, "Right now Ron Sider is dropping pro-life bombs all over #EFL2016. If you are pro-life, you need to listen humbly," Twitter, January 26, 2016, 10:44 p.m., https://twitter.com/MatthewJHall/status/690198283034181632; Russell Moore [russellmoore], 2016, "My colleague David Platt and I enjoyed being with Dr. and Mrs. Ronald Sider. Dr. Sider's writings on hunger influenced both of us.," Instagram, January 21, 2016, https://www.instagram.com/p/BA0rDEQTMWS.

14 "Christians for Biblical Equality President to Teach Class on Gender Equality and Christianity," PRWeb, January 31, 2016, https://www.prweb.com/releases/2016/01/prweb13191511.htm.; CBE International. "CBE's Mission and Values," Accessed March 12, 2020. https://www.cbeinternational.org/content/cbes-mission.

Russell Moore called Mouw a "friend I've respected all my adult life" who has done "some masterful scholarly work on the nature of the Kingdom."[15] Bruce Ashford, the former provost at Southeastern Baptist Theological Seminary, stated in his 2015 book, *One Nation Under God*, "I am especially indebted to Richard Mouw, whose writings have helped me understand what public faithfulness might look like in an increasingly plural and post-Christian America."[16] No one, however, carries Mouw's influence farther than Tim Keller, a popular author, former pastor of Redeemer Presbyterian Church in New York City, and co-founder of The Gospel Coalition, who repeatedly cites Mouw in his works.[17]

Like Mouw, Keller also pursued 1960s neo-Marxist ideas in college before returning to Christianity where he found in Abraham Kuyper's writings a blueprint for how Christians should approach social reform.[18] Not surprisingly, Keller saw value in Mouw's teachings on "common grace," which he believed Christians could use not only to "build up the church through evangelism and discipleship, but also to be deeply involved in cultural activity, as philosophers, art critics, filmmakers, journalists, [and] social theorists."[19] In a 2006 talk for Redeemer Presbyterian's Entrepreneurship Initiative, Keller quoted Mouw as stating, "God is a venture capitalist." He went on to articulate a message reminiscent of Mouw's argument in *Political Evangelism*. Keller

15 Russell Moore, "My Top 10 Books of 2016," December 6, 2016. https://www.russellmoore.com/2016/12/06/top-10-books-2016/; Russell Moore, "The Evangelical Conscience: Still Uneasy After All These Years," September 17, 2003. https://www.russellmoore.com/2003/09/17/the-evangelical-conscience-still-uneasy-after-all-these-years.

16 Bruce Ashford, and Chris Pappalardo, *One Nation Under God: A Christian Hope for American Politics*, B&H Publishing Group, 2015, 2.

17 Tim Keller, *Generous Justice: How God's Grace Makes Us Just* (Penguin Publishing Group, 2012), 221, 160; Tim Keller, *Gospel in Life Study Guide: Grace Changes Everything* (Zondervan, 2013), 143; Tim Keller, *Cultural Engagement: Center Church, Part Five* (Zondervan, 2013); Tim Keller, *Every Good Endeavor: Connecting Your Work to God's Work* (Penguin Publishing Group, 2014), 50-51, 289.

18 Tim Keller, *The Reason for God: Belief in an Age of Skepticism* (Penguin Publishing Group, 2008), xi-xii; Keller, *Generous Justice*, 145-146, 215, 222; Keller, *Every Good Endeavor*, 4, 252.

19 Keller, *Generous Justice*, 221.

asserted, "The whole purpose of salvation is to cleanse and purify this material world."[20]

Mouw's cordial personality, academic achievement, and popular influence make him today's most widely respected member of the original evangelical left. His endorsement is sought after by more progressive leaning evangelical authors like Tim Keller, Karen Swallow Prior, John Fea, Michael Wear, and Alan Noble.[21] Influential evangelicals, like church growth pioneers Bill Hybels and Rick Warren, to academics like historian Mark Noll, to institutional leaders like Mark Galli, have also endorsed Mouw's writings.[22]

Though more activist than academic, John Perkins also enjoys wide acclaim in the evangelical community. In recent years he has spoken for the ERLC and The Gospel Coalition, as well as Southern Seminary and Wheaton College. Southern Baptist pastor Mark Dever, founder of 9 Marks ministries, agreed with Perkins' critique of evangelicalism's departure from the true gospel of "reconciling power."[23] Tim Keller re-branded Perkins' concept of "redistribution" by calling it "reweaving a community" in his best-selling work, *Generous Justice.*[24]

In 2014, Perkins collaborated with other evangelicals like pastors John Piper and Matt Chandler in *Letters to a Birmingham Jail*. Perkins' chapter

---

20 Tim Keller, "Cultural Renewal: The Role of the Intrapreneur and the Entrepreneur" (Entrepreneurship Forum, Lamb's Ballroom, Times Square, March 25, 2006), 4:30, 9. https://web.archive.org/web/20060622051746/http://www.faithandwork.org/uploads/photos/461-1%20Cultural%20Renewal_%20The%20Role%20of%20th.mp3.

21 Tim Keller and John Inazu, *Uncommon Ground: Living Faithfully in a World of Difference* (Thomas Nelson, 2020), Back Cover; Karen Swallow Prior, *Fierce Convictions: The Extraordinary Life of Hannah More? Poet, Reformer, Abolitionist* (Thomas Nelson, 2014), Back Cover; John Fea, *Believe Me: The Evangelical Road to Donald Trump* (Wm. B. Eerdmans Publishing, 2018); Michael Wear, *Reclaiming Hope: Lessons Learned in the Obama White House About the Future of Faith in America* (Thomas Nelson, 2017), Back Cover; Alan Noble, *Disruptive Witness: Speaking Truth in a Distracted Age* (InterVarsity Press, 2018), Back Cover.

22 Richard Mouw, *Consulting the Faithful: What Christian Intellectuals Can Learn from Popular Religion*, (Wm. B. Eerdmans Publishing), 1994. Back Cover; Richard Mouw, *Praying at Burger King* (Wm. B. Eerdmans Publishing), 2007. Back Cover; Richard Mouw and Douglas A. Sweeney, *The Suffering and Victorious Christ: Toward a More Compassionate Christology* (Baker Academic, 2013), Back Cover; Mouw, *Restless Faith*, Back Cover.

23 Mark Dever, "How to Kill a Church," https://www.desiringgod.org/messages/gospel-purity/excerpts/how-to-kill-a-church.

24 Tim Keller, *Generous Justice*, 120.

was on economic justice. In 2017, he spoke alongside Russell Moore at the "Courageous Conversations Conference" hosted by Word Tabernacle Church in Rocky Mount, North Carolina. The *Tennessee Star* described: "The focus of the one-day conference is on race, but an emphasis on economic redistribution is interwoven with the activists' teachings."[25] Perkins' 1982 book *With Justice For All*, which sought to "champion an alternative" between "atheistic communism" and "capitalism," is used today by Cru's (formerly Campus Crusade) Urban Project Los Angeles as a framework for exploring his "three Rs: relocation, reconciliation, and redistribution."[26]

At The Gospel Coalition's MLK50 conference in 2018, Perkins described well the changing perception mainstream evangelicals had of him, and indeed progressive evangelicals in general. He stated, "When Martin Luther King was doing his march on Washington and all that, we was communists. And I never would have thought that I would have lived to see us tonight looking like we are looking tonight."[27] The activist from Mississippi who made his evangelical debut writing for *The Other Side* and *Sojourners* had come a long way. So had evangelical Christianity. And no one from the evangelical left had come farther politically than Jim Wallis.

Brantley Gasaway observed that if Ron Sider was the "pastor" of the evangelical left, Jim Wallis was its "prophet."[28] Though some current left leaning mainstream evangelicals like Karen Swallow Prior, Ed Stetzer, and Jemar Tisby have all written for *Sojourners*, Wallis rarely, if ever, writes for evangelical outlets considered mainstream. Most theologically conservative

25 Wendy Wilson, "Southern Baptist ERLC's Russell Moore Collaborating with Christians Who Promote Wealth Redistribution, Amnesty for Illegal Immigrants," *Tennessee Star*, September 12, 2017, https://tennesseestar.com/2017/09/12/southern-baptist-erlcs-russell-moore-collaborating-with-christians-who-promote-wealth-redistribution-amnesty-for-illegal-immigrants.

26 John Perkins, *With Justice for All* (Ventura, CA: Regal Books, 1982), 168; "The Three R's," Urban Project - Los Angeles, accessed May 2, 2020, http://www.urbanprojectinternational.com/contact.

27 John Perkins, *The Civil Rights Movement 50 Years after MLK* (MLK 50 Conference: The Gospel Coalition, 2018), https://youtu.be/q8KVSjrUqHo.

28 Gasaway, *Progressive Evangelicals and the Pursuit of Social Justice*, 16.

evangelicals have little positive to say about Wallis publicly. Stephen Nichols, a popular evangelical author, chief academic officer at Ligonier ministries, and president of Reformation Bible College, is an exception.

Nichols praised Wallis in his 2008 book, *Jesus Made in America*. From Nichols' perspective, "Jim Wallis . . . made a fairly good case that there are issues on the right that would be difficult to connect to Jesus."[29] Wallis, he said, made a "profound observation" concerning conservatives who attribute poverty to immorality by calling them "mean" and "stupid."[30] In warning about the negative impact of "consumer culture and its dehumanizing and oppressive effects on both people and ecology," Nichols lauded Wallis' "community economics" which cut "against Western capitalism and 'market economics.'"[31]

Because of his more militant public presence, Wallis' influence in mainstream evangelicalism is substantially less than his political influence. In 2007, he hosted John Edwards, Barack Obama, and Hillary Clinton in a presidential forum sponsored by Sojourners and broadcast on CNN.[32] Wallis became one of Barack Obama's five spiritual advisors in 2009, though he had known the president since the 1990s.[33] *The Daily Beast* referred to him in 2011 as the "face of progressive Christianity in Washington."[34]

In recent years, Wallis, along with other 1970s era progressive evangelicals, have partnered with leaders in mainstream evangelicalism to accomplish shared social and political objectives. In 2007, a statement on Christianity and Islam called "A Common Word," highlighted similarities between the Quran and the New Testament surrounding love for God and neighbor. Progressive

29 Stephen Nichols, *Jesus Made in America: A Cultural History from the Puritans to "The Passion of the Christ"* (InterVarsity Press, 2008), loc 2621-2622, Kindle Edition.
30 Ibid., loc 2423-2426.
31 Ibid., loc 2320-2324.
32 "Sojourners Presidential Forum," CNN, June 4, 2007, http://transcripts.cnn.com/TRAN-SCRIPTS/0706/04/sitroom.03.html.
33 Laurie Goodstein, "Without a Pastor of His Own, Obama Turns to Five," *The New York Times*, March 14, 2009, sec. U.S., https://www.nytimes.com/2009/03/15/us/politics/15pastor.html.
34 David Sessions, "Liberal Christians Attack Obama Spiritual Adviser Jim Wallis over Gay Ad," *The Daily Beast*, May 10, 2011, https://www.thedailybeast.com/articles/2011/05/10/liberal-christians-attack-obama-spiritual-adviser-jim-wallis-over-gay-ad.

evangelicals, including Wes Granberg-Michaelson, Richard Mouw, and Jim Wallis endorsed the statement, along with David Neff, Vice-President of Christianity Today Media Group, Leith Anderson, the president of the National Association of Evangelicals, and pastors Rick Warren and Bill Hybels.[35]

Jim Wallis helped launch the Evangelical Immigration Table in 2012, along with mainstream evangelicals like Richard Land, Russell Moore's predecessor at the ERLC, and Tom Minnery of Focus on the Family.[36] Richard Mouw, Ron Sider, and John Perkins also signed on to the organization, which is dedicated to the establishment of a lawful "path toward legal status" for qualified undocumented migrants.[37] Though many other mainstream evangelicals endorsed the project, Wallis along with Russell Moore, Leith Anderson, and Stephan Bauman, the President of World Relief, are regularly featured contributors.[38]

In 2015, after the Obergefell v Hodges Supreme Court decision affirming same-sex marriage, Richard Mouw and Ron Sider joined prominent Southern Baptists to sign an ERLC statement supporting "the enduring truth that marriage consists of one man and one woman."[39] Some pioneers of the evangelical left, like Jim Wallis, Virginia Ramey Mollenkott and Wes Granberg-Michaelson, supported same sex marriage.[40] However, Mouw and

---

35 "'A Common Word' Christian Response," Yale Center for Faith and Culture, accessed May 1, 2020, https://faith.yale.edu/common-word/common-word-christian-response.

36 Jack Palmer, "Evangelical Leaders Announce Immigration Table Launch," *Sojourners*, June 12, 2012, https://sojo.net/articles/evangelical-leaders-announce-immigration-table-launch.

37 "About," Evangelical Immigration Table, accessed May 1, 2020, http://evangelicalimmigrationtable.com/about.

38 "Letters Urges Congress, Administration: Welcome Refugees," Evangelical Immigration Table, October 1, 2015, http://evangelicalimmigrationtable.com/letters-urges-congress-administration-welcome-refugees.

39 "Here We Stand: An Evangelical Declaration on Marriage," *Christianity Today*, June 26, 2015, https://www.christianitytoday.com/ct/2015/june-web-only/here-we-stand-evangelical-declaration-on-marriage.html.

40 Jaweed Kaleem, "Jim Wallis Talks Faith's Role In Politics, Gay Marriage And Immigration," *Huffington Post*, April 5, 2013, https://www.huffpost.com/entry/jim-wallis-faith-politics-immigration_n_3024458; Virginia Ramey Mollenkott and Richard Mouw, "Gay Marriage: Broken or Blessed? Two Evangelical Views," interview by Krista Tippett, August 3, 2006, https://onbeing.org/programs/richard-mouw-and-virginia-ramey-mollenkott-gay-marriage-broken-or-blessed-two-evangelical-views/; James V. Brownson, Bible, Gender, Sexuality: Reframing the Church's Debate on Same-Sex Relationships (Wm. B. Eerdmans Publishing, 2013).

Sider, along with mainstream evangelicals, still believed exclusively in heterosexual marriage. Their attitudes on homosexuality were softening, though.

Richard Mouw held the same position as many on the Christian Right but he opposed evangelicalism's past "sexually oppressive subculture" and placed homosexual actions on the same moral level as failing to show "concern for the poor" and supporting "anti-immigrant policies."[41] Ron Sider thought "Christians who openly acknowledge a gay orientation" should "commit themselves to celibacy." Yet, he also believed that churches should be places where an "openly, unabashedly gay, celibate Christian" should "find love, support, and full affirmation of gifts."[42] For mainstream evangelicals, the concept of "gay Christians" was new, let alone the idea of letting them serve in ministry capacities.

The 2016 election afforded progressive evangelicals more access into the mainstream than they previously enjoyed. Leading up to the election, "A Declaration by American Evangelicals Concerning Donald Trump" opposed the Republican candidate's "racial, religious, and gender bigotry." Jim Wallis, Ron Sider, and Wes Granberg-Michaelson joined with other popular names like David Neff, author Rachel Held Evans, and Jemar Tisby, the president of the Reformed African American Network, in signing.[43]

After Donald Trump won with eighty-nine percent of the evangelical vote, many evangelical elites wanted to separate themselves from his supporters.[44] Mouw informed *Christianity Today*, after the election, that his

---

41 Chad Thompson, *Loving Homosexuals as Jesus Would: A Fresh Christian Approach* (Brazos Press, 2004), 91; Richard Mouw and Nathaniel Frank, "What Do We Really Think About Homosexuality?", interview by Neal Conan, March 21, 2007, https://www.npr.org/templates/story/story.php?storyId=9041745.

42 Ron Sider, "Tragedy, Tradition, and Opportunity in the Homosexuality Debate," *Christianity Today*, November 18, 2014, https://www.christianitytoday.com/ct/2014/november-web-only/ron-sider-tragedy-tradition-and-opportunity-in-homosexualit.html; It should be noted that Ron Sider had also signed the "Manhattan Declaration" in 2009, which advocated "civil disobedience" if governing authorities were to compel Christians to violate biblical teaching on life and sexuality. See Manhattan Declaration, "Manhattan Declaration: A Call to Christian Conscience," Manhattan Declaration, November 20, 2009, https://www.manhattandeclaration.org.

43 "A Declaration by American Evangelicals Concerning Donald Trump," Change.org, 2016, https://www.change.org/p/donald-trump-a-declaration-by-american-evangelicals-concerning-donald-trump.

44 Amy Julia Becker, "Why I Am Ditching the Label 'Evangelical' in the Trump Era,"

"feelings" bordered "on despair."[45] Jim Wallis told the *Chicago Sun Times,* "There is a conflict between the politics of Jesus and the politics of Trump."[46] In 2017, World Relief purchased space in the *Washington Post* for a statement from "Evangelical Leaders" urging "President Trump to Reconsider Reduction in Refugee Resettlement." Signers included John Perkins, Richard Mouw, and mainstream evangelicals like Tim Keller, Ed Stetzer, the Director of The Wheaton College Billy Graham Center, and Daniel Akin, the President of Southeastern Baptist Theological Seminary.[47] The next year, around "50 evangelical Christian leaders," including Jim Wallis, Tim Keller, Mark Noll, and Trillia Newbell, the director of community outreach for the ERLC, gathered at Wheaton College to discuss their concern that evangelicalism had "become too closely associated with President Trump's polarizing politics."[48]

In 2019, the AND Campaign, led by two *Christianity Today* contributors, Michael Wear, one of President Obama's faith advisors, and Justin Giboney, a Democrat political strategist, produced a "2020 Presidential Election Statement" to "promote social justice and moral order." Both Richard Mouw and Ron Sider were among the prominent signatories.[49]

On March 31, 2020, the Asian American Christian Collaborative released a "Statement on Anti-Asian Racism in the Time of COVID-19." Its purpose was to combat "anti-Asian racism" through speaking, teaching "Asian-American histories of oppression," providing "culturally-competent mental health services" for Asian-Americans "in all public schools," supporting "Asian

Washington Post, October 18, 2017, https://www.washingtonpost.com/news/acts-of-faith/wp/2017/10/18/why-i-am-ditching-the-label-evangelical-in-the-trump-era.

45 Compiled by Emily Lund, "Trump Won. Here's How 20 Evangelical Leaders Feel.," *Christianity Today,* November 11, 2016, https://www.christianitytoday.com/ct/2016/november-web-only/trump-won-how-evangelical-leaders-feel.html.

46 Neil Steinberg, "Trump v. Jesus: Christians Can't Follow Both," *Chicago Sun-Times,* October 10, 2019, https://chicago.suntimes.com/columnists/2019/10/10/20908102/trump-jesus-christians-evangelicals-religion-jim-wallis-steinberg.

47 "Evangelical Leaders from All 50 States Urge President Trump to Reconsider Reduction in Refugee Resettlement," *The Washington Post,* February 3, 2017, sec. A18.

48 Emily McFarlan Miller, "Evangelical Leaders Gather at Wheaton to Discuss Future of the Movement in Trump Era," *Sojourners,* April 17, 2018, https://sojo.net/articles/evangelical-leaders-gather-wheaton-discuss-future-movement-trump-era.

49 "AND Campaign," AND Campaign, accessed May 1, 2020, https://andcampaign.org.

businesses . . . disproportionately . . . impacted by COVID-19," and holding politicians "accountable for 'harmful rhetoric'" while encouraging them to seek the "common good." The statement described these objectives as "gospel driven work."[50] Hundreds of mainstream evangelical leaders signed, including the heads of InterVarsity Press, InterVarsity Christian Fellowship, *Christianity Today*, Navigators, the National Association of Evangelicals, and the Billy Graham Center for Evangelism at Wheaton. Their names, along with those of popular evangelical pastors like Thabiti Anyabwile, Matt Chandler, and Derwin Gray appeared beside Nikki Toyama-Szeto, the Executive Director of Evangelicals for Social Action, Ron Sider, Richard Mouw, and Jim Wallis.[51] Mainstream evangelicals were not only partnering with 1970s era progressive evangelicals, they were also speaking their language.

After the death of George Floyd on May 25, 2020, Black Lives Matter, an organization started in 2013 by self-described "trained Marxists" for the purpose of "creating a world free of anti-Blackness," the "Western-prescribed nuclear family," "heteronormative thinking," "ageism," "cis-gender privilege," "violence," "sexism," and "misogyny," sponsored antiracist protest marches across the United States.[52] Evangelical leaders like Ed Stetzer and megachurch pastor Joel Osteen, took part in some of the protests, while pastors David Platt and Thabiti Anyabwile helped organize a more Christian styled march in support of the movement.[53] Many mainstream evangelical organizations,

---

50 Asian American Christian Collaborative, "Statement on Anti-Asian Racism in the Time of COVID-19." Accessed April 8, 2020. https://asianamericanchristiancollaborative. com/covid19statement.

51 Asian American Christian Collaborative,"Signed by Institutions," Accessed April 8, 2020, https://asianamericanchristiancollaborative.com/signatories-of-institutions; Asian American Christian Collaborative, "Signed by Friends of the Asian American Community," Accessed April 8, 2020, https://asianamericanchristiancollaborative. com/signed-by-friends.

52 Yaron Steinbuch, "Black Lives Matter Co-Founder Describes Herself as 'Trained Marxist,'" *New York Post*, June 25, 2020, https://nypost.com/2020/06/25/blm-co-founder-describes-herself-as-trained-marxist; "What We Believe," Black Lives Matter, accessed July 14, 2020, https://blacklivesmatter.com/what-we-believe.

53 Diana Chandler, "Baptists Join Diverse Group of Faith Leaders in Chicago March," *Biblical Recorder*, June 4, 2020, https://www.brnow.org/news/baptists-join-diverse-group-of-faith-leaders-in-chicago-march/; Zachary Halaschak, "'This Is Not a Political Issue': Joel Osteen Says Floyd Death 'Ignited Something in Me,'" *Washington*

including the Southern Baptist Convention, Cru, and World Vision also issued statements denouncing systemic racial injustice.[54] The president of the Southern Baptist Convention, J.D. Greear, denounced the organization Black Lives Matter, but still maintained that the slogan, which called for examining "police systems," "listening," and "lamenting," was a "gospel issue."[55]

Much of the rhetoric surrounding the sudden concern over historic injustices and systemic oppression sounded very similar to the kind of language used in the 1970s by Tom Skinner, John Alexander, and of course, Jim Wallis. In fact, Wallis supported the Black Lives Matter movement since 2014 and in 2016, he sat on a panel with Alicia Garza, one of the three founders of the organization, telling her that her work "struck at the heart of America's original sin" which was the "founding principle" that "indigenous lives and black lives don't matter."[56] Language, which at one time was regarded as political and divisive by mainstream evangelicals, was now considered religious and unifying.

Today, a new generation of evangelicals promoting progressive values is on the horizon. Books like *Woke Church* (2018) by Eric Mason and *Color of Compromise* (2019) by Jemar Tisby are making their own dent for "racial

Examiner, June 10, 2020, https://www.washingtonexaminer.com/news/this-is-not-a-political-issue-joel-osteen-says-floyd-death-ignited-something-in-me.; Jack Jenkins, "Mitt Romney Joins Evangelical Racial Justice March in DC," News & Reporting, June 7, 2020, https://www.christianitytoday.com/news/2020/june/mitt-romney-dc-march-thabiti-anyabwile-christians.html.

54 "Southern Baptist Leaders Issue Joint Statement on the Death of George Floyd," *Baptist Press*, accessed July 14, 2020, http://www.bpnews.net/54877/southern-baptist-leaders-issue-joint-statement-on-the-death-of-george-floyd; Milton Massie, "Naming Sin: A Response to the Killing of George Floyd" Cru, accessed July 14, 2020, https://www.cru.org/us/en/communities/innercity/media/naming-sin.html; Andrew Morley, "Statement on Ending Racial Injustice," World Vidsion, June 11, 2020, https://www.wvi.org/newsroom/statement-ending-racial-injustice.

55 Leonardo Blair, "JD Greear Endorses Black Lives Matter as Gospel Issue, Denounces Organization," *The Christian Post*, June 10, 2020, https://www.christianpost.com/news/jd-greear-endorses-black-lives-matter-as-gospel-issue-denounces-blm-organization.html.

56 Jim Wallis, *America's Original Sin: Racism, White Privilege, and the Bridge to a New America* (Brazos Press, 2016), 134; Jim Wallis et al., *The Movement Moment - Panel at CitizenUCon16*, interview by Eric Liu, March 18, 2016, 26:50. https://www.youtube.com/watch?v=iF9AxqX5yYg.

justice."[57] *Generous Justice* (2012) by Tim Keller and *Onward* (2015) by Russell Moore promote a more general vision of the "common good." *Recovering from Biblical Manhood and Womanhood* (2020) by Aimee Byrd and *Fierce, Free, and Full of Fire* (2020) by Jen Hatmaker challenge traditional patriarchy.[58] *Crazy Love* (2008) by Francis Chan and *Radical* (2010) by David Platt both promote simple living.[59]

Mainstream evangelicals are now talking about the idolatrous dangers of nationalism, how churches can be more inclusive to racial minorities, women, and same-sex attracted people, and how Christians should mobilize to protest social injustice and promote the redistribution of privilege and resources for the benefit of the oppressed. Some terms have changed. "Equity" is replacing "equality," "Human flourishing" has substituted "common good," and "woke," instead of Wallis' term, "radical awakening," describes gaining an understanding of oppression and disparities.[60] Still, the basic New Left concepts which motivated progressive evangelicals of the 1970s are making their way into the heart of the evangelical movement. The prophets for social concern are accomplishing their mission, though much later than they originally wanted to.

If mainstream evangelicals continue down the path of embracing New Left ideas from the 1960s, it will mean the end of evangelicalism's politically conservative character. Because of the larger percentages of evangelicals residing in Southern and Midwestern states, the electoral map will potentially

---

57 John Perkins wrote a forward for *Woke Church*; Evangelicals for Social Action endorsed *Color of Compromise*. See Rose Adriel, "For Those With Ears to Hear: A Review of 'The Color of Compromise,'" Evangelicals for Social Action, March 13, 2019, https://www.evangelicalsforsocialaction.org/resources/book-reviews/ears-hear-review-color-compromise.

58 Sojourners promoted Jen Hatmaker. See Emily McFarlan Miller, "Christian Author Jen Hatmaker on the 'Moxie' It Takes to Get Your Books Banned," *Sojourners*, August 7, 2017, https://sojo.net/articles/christian-author-jen-hatmaker-moxie-it-takes-get-your-books-banned.

59 *The Christian Post* published: "Platt's arguments aren't new. Ron Sider's book Rich Christians in an Age of Hunger: Moving from Affluence to Generosity released decades ago and is now in its fifth edition." See "Will 'Radical' Christianity Have Any Effect on the American Church?," *Christian Post*, September 17, 2010, https://www.christianpost.com/news/will-radical-christianity-have-any-effect-on-the-american-church.html.

60 Wallis, "Post-American Christianity."

become more difficult for Republican candidates unless they are able to tap into another demographic or move to the left. Political pundits are starting to recognize the leftward trend among today's young evangelicals, but only time will tell if the current movement makes a significant lasting difference.

One concern some social observers have is a fear that churches and Christian organizations will serve as off-ramps from Christianity itself. Recently, Ekemini Uwan, a popular evangelical social justice advocate tweeted, "Some of y'all are decolonizing your faith to the point that you're decolonizing your way out of the faith."[61] If younger evangelicals become convinced their own religious tradition is characterized by bigotry, they may leave. In a multicultural and transitory world of countless options, churches already have significantly less holding power than they did when Wallis and Sider started their organizations.

Conversely, older more traditional evangelicals may leave churches and ministries, or stop funding them, over theological disagreements with a broader more politically progressive understanding of the gospel. In recent years, many mainstream evangelical elites have almost caught up with the progressive views of the 1970s-era leaders who inspired them. Working class Christians who fund much of evangelicalism may not be as quick to adopt New Left understandings.

If anything is certain for the future of evangelicalism, it is that lasting changes are happening now. The most important question for Christians themselves is if they will be able to hold on to their orthodoxy while combining their faith tradition with ideas stemming from neo-Marxist ideology. The myriad of empty churches belonging to mainline denominations in the United States are monuments to what can happen when a social gospel, which downplays defining Christian doctrines, replaces the personal message of Christ's sacrifice for individuals.

---

61 Ekemini Uwan [@sista_theology], 2020 Twitter, "Some of y'all are decolonizing your faith to the point that you're decolonizing your way out of the faith," Twitter, July 2, 2020, 9:32 a.m., https://twitter.com/sista_theology/status/1278682997320036354.

Progressive pioneers like Jim Wallis, Wes Granberg-Michaelson, Sharon Gallagher, John Alexander, Richard Mouw, Ron Sider, and John Perkins all integrated their political views with their Christian faith. Through a long and, at times, discouraging process, their version of Christianity is now a major driving force within evangelicalism. However, what they created in the 1970s is now outside of their control. As the baton is passed to a new generation, one wonders if their children will carry on the progressive Christianity of their youth, or, like their parents and grandparents before them, form a still different kind of evangelicalism.

TIM KELLER AND PROGRESSIVE EVANGELICALISM

PERHAPS NO ONE HAS DONE more to narrow the gap between progressive evangelicalism and mainstream evangelicalism than Tim Keller. Keller grew up in a mainline Lutheran church. As a teenager, during confirmation class, a young Lutheran cleric and social activist introduced him to a Christian version of social liberation grounded in a "spirit of love." However, the Kellers soon started attending a conservative Methodist church which helped reinforce their son's more traditional conception of God and the reality of hell.[1] What he could not harmonize as a teenager—the ethics of the New Left and orthodox Christianity—he started learning to reconcile in college.

While attending Bucknell University, in his home state of Pennsylvania, Keller learned the "reigning ideologies of the time" from radical professors, including the "neo-Marxist critical theory of the Frankfurt School."[2] He was attracted to this "critique of American bourgeoisie society," as well as social activism. Keller described himself and fellow students as wanting to "change the world" by rejecting things like "the military-industrial complex" and "a society of inequities and materialism." Instead, they promoted "peace and

---

1 Tim Keller, *The Reason for God: Belief in an Age of Skepticism,* (New York: Dutton, 2008), xi.
2 Tim Keller, February 14, 1993, "Let Your Yes Be Yes," *The Timothy Keller Sermon Archive* (New York City: Redeemer Presbyterian Church, 2013); Keller, May 2, 1993, "House of God—Part 3," *The Timothy Keller Sermon Archive*; Keller, *The Reason for God*, xi.

understanding," attended peace and civil rights marches, and shut down the college to debate the morality of the Cambodian invasion in 1970.[3] Though things like segregation and "systemic violence . . . against blacks" bothered Keller before college, they became an occasion for him to doubt Christianity itself after his arrival.[4]

It was hard enough for the young student to maintain his faith while regularly hearing philosophical objections to it, living a "double life," and struggling with deep depression.[5] There were times he wondered if he was "just a cog in a machine" determined by his environment.[6] However, the "spiritual crisis" he experienced as a student was also the result of a tension between his more activist "secular friends" and Christians who considered Martin Luther King, Jr., to be a social threat.[7] Keller had a dilemma.

While he was emotionally drawn to "social justice," its practitioners were "moral relativists" who could not ground their convictions in an objective standard. When Christian evangelist John Guest came to campus and boldly challenged protestors for their inability to morally reason, Keller was there.[8] At the same time, he was disenchanted with "orthodox Christianity" which he believed supported things like segregation and apartheid.[9] Fortunately, for Keller, the evangelical left offered a version of the faith which married the ethics of the New Left with the metaphysical foundation Christianity provided. He began to realize he could have both.

3 Keller, August, 26, 1990, "The Secret Siege of Nineveh," *The Timothy Keller Sermon Archive*; Keller, March 15, 1992, "Missions," *The Timothy Keller Sermon Archive*; Keller, May 1, 1994, "Who is This Jesus?," The *Timothy Keller Sermon Archive*.

4 Tim Keller, *Generous Justice How God's Grace Makes Us Just*, (East Rutherford: Penguin Publishing Group, 2010), loc 151-160, Kindle.

5 Keller, May 27, 1990, "Christian Experience & Counterfeit," *The Timothy Keller Sermon Archive*; Keller, February 5, 1995, "Loving and Growing—Part 2," *The Timothy Keller Sermon Archive*. Keller, September 3, 1989, "Politics of the King," *The Timothy Keller Sermon Archive*.

6 Keller, October 7, 1990, "Spiritual Gifts—Part3," *The Timothy Keller Sermon Archive*.

7 Tim Keller, *Encounters with Jesus Unexpected Answers to Life's Biggest Questions* (East Rutherford: Penguin Publishing Group, 2013), xv; Keller, *Generous Justice*, loc 160-167.

8 Keller, March 25, 1990, "Goodness and Faithfulness," *The Timothy Keller Sermon Archive*.

9 Keller, *The Reason for God*, xii.

Keller wrote that things began to change for him after finding a "band of brothers" who grounded their concern for justice in the character of God.[10] He became part of a "campus fellowship" sponsored by InterVarsity which reflected the counterculture mindset of Bucknell by keeping their ministry non-traditional, "spontaneous," and anti-institutional. It was there Keller first truly "came to Christ."[11] He also learned to navigate the cultural battle between people against "commie pinkos" "rabble-rousing in the street" and the radicals who protested on those streets.

In 1970, Keller heard a message which revolutionized his approach to political issues. Some of his friends attended InterVarsity's Missions Conference called "Urbana 70" where the Harlem evangelist, Tom Skinner, spoke about a "revolutionary" Jesus who was incompatible with "Americanism."[12] Skinner taught that the evangelical church had upheld slavery in the nation's political, economic, and religious systems. While greedy landlords paid off corrupt building inspectors, police forces maintained the "interests of white society," and the top one percent controlled the entire economy, evangelicals were silent and even supported the "industrial complex."[13] The twenty-year-old Keller already resonated with the New Left critique, but Skinner's way of incorporating it into Christianity was new for him.

His friends gave him a tape recording of Skinner's talk and Keller "could not listen to this sermon enough."[14] Skinner claimed that a "gospel" that did not "speak to the issue of enslavement," "injustice," or "inequality" was "not the gospel." Instead, he fused the incomplete gospels of both "fundamentalists" and "liberals" into a salvation which delivered from both personal and systemic evil. Jesus had come "to change the system" and Christians were to preach

---

10 Ibid., xii.
11 Keller, August 5, 1990, "Blueprint for Revival: Introduction—Part 2," *The Timothy Keller Sermon Archive.*
12 Keller, February 23, 1997, "With a Politician," *The Timothy Keller Sermon Archive.*
13 Tom Skinner, "The U.S. Racial Crisis and World Evangelism," (Speech delivered at Urbana Student Missions Conference, Urbana, Illinois, 1970). https://urbana.org/message/us-racial-crisis-and-world-evangelism.
14 Keller, "With a Politician."

"liberation to oppressed people."[15] The sermon astounded Keller. It was just the kind of reconciliation he was waiting for and it left him unable to "think about politics the same way again" after hearing it.[16] Tom Skinner, however, was not the only voice which helped Keller cultivate New Left ideas in Christian soil.

After graduating from Bucknell, Keller worked for InterVarsity Christian Fellowship in Boston, Massachusetts, and attended Gordon-Conwell Theological Seminary where he met fellow seminarian Elward Ellis. Ellis was a student leader for InterVarsity and had previously been a "key leader in recruiting black students to attend Urbana 70 through a film that he wrote and produced" entitled, "What Went Down at Urbana 67."[17] The film challenged the notion that missions was "Christian racism" and promoted the idea that those of non-European descent could "preach the gospel the way it should be," instead of the "honkified way of preaching the gospel."[18] Carl Ellis, an InterVarsity leader who had "enlisted Tom Skinner as a speaker" for the event, narrated the video.[19] Like Skinner, Elward Ellis also imported New Left thinking into Christianity.

Ellis introduced Keller to concepts now referred to as "systemic racism" and "white privilege" by showing him that "white folks did not have to be personally bigoted . . . in order to support social, educational, judicial, and economic systems and customs that automatically privileged whites over others."[20] On one occasion Ellis called Keller a "racist" even though he admitted that Keller didn't "mean to be" or "want to be." Ellis told Keller that he simply could not "really help it" since Keller was blind to his own "cultural biases" which he used to judge "people of other races."[21] White Christians, Ellis main-

15 Skinner, "The U.S. Racial Crisis and World Evangelism."
16 Keller, March 11, 2007, "Jesus and Politics," *The Timothy Keller Sermon Archive.*
17 Gordon Govier, "In Remembrance – Elward Ellis," InterVarsity, May 14, 2012, https://intervarsity.org/news/remembrance-%E2%80%93-elward-ellis.
18 "What Went Down at Urbana 67 - Urbana 70 Black Student Promotional," (Ken Anderson Films), accessed August 15, 2020, 2:30, 13:05, https://vimeo.com/42230364.
19 David Swartz, *Moral Minority: The Evangelical Left in an Age of Conservatism* (University of Pennsylvania Press, 2012), loc 573-581, Kindle.
20 Irwyn Ince Jr, *The Beautiful Community: Unity, Diversity, and the Church at Its Best* (InterVarsity Press, 2020), 2.
21 Keller, *Generous Justice,* loc 168-180.

tained, practiced discrimination by making their "cultural preferences," such as singing and preaching styles, "normative for everyone." White people, in general, were also ignorant of the hardships racial minorities underwent in navigating "Euro-white culture."[22] Keller gladly accepted Ellis' "bare-knuckled mentoring about the realities of injustice in American culture."[23] He now understood, in greater detail, certain aspects of the New Left critique, but still needed to further develop a Christian response to the unjust status quo. But first, he needed a job.

In 1975, Tim Keller married his wife Kathy at the beginning of his final semester at Gordon-Conwell. After graduation, he was ordained in the Presbyterian Church of America (PCA) and moved to Virginia where he pastored a church in a "blue collar, Southern town." He also served as a regional director of church planting for the PCA. Somehow, in the midst of his busy schedule, Keller also managed to take courses from Westminster Theological Seminary where he earned a Doctor of Ministry degree in 1981. Three years later, he moved to Philadelphia to take a job teaching at Westminster.[24] It was there he met Harvie Conn, a professor of missions who helped Keller take the next step in marrying his social justice concerns with his Christian faith.

Some considered Conn a "bit of a radical" for challenging the interpretations of "white Presbyterian males" based on their allegedly biased cultural presuppositions.[25] Instead, he believed in a "contextual approach" he referred to as a "hermeneutical spiral" for interpreting the Bible. This approach combined interpretation and application by emphasizing "the cultural contexts of

---

22 Tim Keller, forward to *The Beautiful Community: Unity, Diversity, and the Church at Its Best*, 3.

23 Keller, *Generous Justice*, loc 168-180.

24 Keller, October 31, 1993, "The Battle for the Heart," *The Tim Keller Sermon Archive*; "Tim Keller," Cruciformity Shaped By The Cross: Christian Life Conference 2007, February 18, 2007, https://web.archive.org/web/20070218113355/http://clc.2pc.org/index.php/tim-keller.

25 Peter Enns, "The (Or at Least 'A') Problem with Evangelical White Churches," *Patheos* (blog), July 2, 2015, https://www.patheos.com/blogs/peterenns/2015/07/the-or-at-least-a-problem-with-evangelical-white-churches/; Mark Gornik, "The Legacy of Harvie M. Conn," *International Bulletin of Missionary Research* 35, no. 4 (October 2011), 214.

the biblical text and the contemporary readers" which called for a "dialogue between the two" in a "dynamic interplay between text and interpreters."[26] Of course, this method of interpretation denied "objectivism" and the "classic pattern of historic-grammatical exegesis." Because "sociological and economic preconceptions" influenced one's interpretation of the Bible and the world, Conn affirmed, along with "liberation theologians," a "need for new input from sociology, economics, and politics in the doing of theology and missions."[27] In short, Conn believed that the experience of social groups helped determine the meaning and application of a text. Not surprisingly, this approach opened the door for new ways of understanding the Bible.

Liberation theology, which used Marxism as an "instrument of social analysis," awakened Conn's own conscience to the realities of oppression. He believed that "a bias toward the poor, the doing of justice, [and] the battle against racism," were necessary starting points for properly interpreting Scripture.[28] After all, Jesus, who Conn described as a "refugee" and "immigrant," "identified with the poor." Therefore, members of His kingdom must also show "solidarity with the poor" in their personal life and social perspective.[29] Instead, White American evangelicals identified with "saints" and required the "world" to come on the church's terms. Not surprisingly, Conn thought "the church must recapture its identity as the only organization in the world that exists for the sake of its nonmembers" and "repent" for things like neglect of the "urban poor," "dull, repetitious, [and] unexciting" services, and hypocrisy.[30]

In order to follow Conn's advice, churches needed to engage in "holistic evangelism," which included working to eliminate "war and poverty and injustice" with a "full gospel" which addressed social questions.[31] Charity alone

---

26 Harvie Conn, "Theologies of Liberation: Toward a Common View," *Tensions in Contemporary Theology*, Third (Moody Press, 1979), 420, 428.
27 Ibid., 413, 421-422.
28 Ibid., 334, 404-405.
29 Ibid., 419-420, 423.
30 Harvie Conn, *Evangelism: Doing Justice and Preaching Grace* (Grand Rapids, Mich: Zondervan Pub. House, 1982), 23-24.
31 Ibid., 56, 73-74.

was not enough.[32] In fact, the gospel possessed its own "political program based on its own analysis of the global reality of man." Conn even believed that "certain socioeconomic commitments [came] closer to certain features of the gospel than others."[33] This broadening of the gospel message and evangelistic task included a fusion of liberation theology, and perhaps Kuyperian thinking, with evangelicalism.[34]

Conn, who disparaged "wealth and whiteness" and compared Wall Street workers with prostitutes, certainly had little affinity for "capitalism," which he believed provided "myths" for understanding "social needs." At the same time, the "Marxist tool" was only useful insofar as it remained subservient to the "Lordship of Christ."[35] Liberation theologians "distorted" the role of the church by "making it into revolution." But, they also challenged the "hidden ideologies" of "conservative evangelicals," such as pietism and privatization, and could help "refine [their] commitment to the gospel." Conn believed the problem with most evangelicals was they gave "the salvation of souls top priority and the concern for social justice only secondary and derived importance."[36] Instead, he pointed to members of the evangelical left such as Orlando Costas, Jim Wallis, John Perkins, Richard Mouw, and Ron Sider as positive examples of evangelicals who understood what the title of his 1982 book, *Evangelism: Doing Justice and Preaching Grace,* promoted.[37]

Tim Keller personally admired Harvie Conn and found his writings to be both "mind-blowing" and deeply impacting.[38] Conn's most famous contributions to missions were his writings on urban ministry. By using insights from "urban sociology, urban anthropology, and biblical theology," Conn showed

---

32 Harvie Conn, *A Clarified Vision for Urban Mission: Dispelling the Urban Stereotypes* (Ministry Resources Library, 1987), 147.
33 Conn, "Theologies of Liberation," 416.
34 Conn, *A Clarified Vision for Urban Mission,* 142, 147.
35 Conn, "Theologies of Liberation," 413-414, 425.
36 Ibid., 413, 409-410, 418.
37 Ibid., 34, 50, 52, 73, 79.
38 Tim Keller, "Westminster - In Memory of Dr. Harvie Conn," Westminster Faculty, August 15, 2000, https://web.archive.org/web/20000815221157/http://www.wts.edu/news/conn.html.

that cities were not the impersonal secular places evangelicals thought them to be.[39] Actually, "the city" carried with it a special eschatological significance. Since the final chapter in human history culminated with the New Jerusalem, it represented a return to Eden. Temporal cities reflected aspects of both Eden and the restoration of Christ as places to "cultivate the earth," "live in safety and security," and "meet God."[40] Scripture taught that Jesus came to "redeem the city," and it was the church's job to join this special "kingdom story."[41] Conn's strategy for evangelizing urban centers involved focusing on social groups, as opposed to individuals, and promoting cross-cultural interactions which served to help eliminate "racism, injustice, and discrimination."[42] Keller resonated with Conn's ideas.

While teaching at Westminster, Keller developed his distinctively Dutch Reformed approach to missions and apologetics under the influence of Conn.[43] The "life-changing impact" Conn had on him manifested itself in 1989 when Keller moved from Philadelphia with his wife and three sons to start Redeemer Presbyterian Church in Manhattan. Keller wrote he would "never, ever, have been open to the idea of church planting in New York City if it were not for the books and example of Harvie Conn."[44] In facing the challenges of urban ministry, Keller appealed to many of Conn's teachings including the priority of cultural contextualization, the hermeneutical spiral, and the eschatological significance of "the city."[45] Like Conn, Keller viewed influencing the city as a way of influencing the broader culture. He accepted Conn's reconfiguration of the "cultural mandate" to fill, subdue,

---

39 Conn, *A Clarified Vision for Urban Mission*, 9-10.
40 Tim Keller, *Loving the City: Doing Balanced, Gospel-Centered Ministry in Your City* (Zondervan, 2016), 310.
41 Gornik, "The Legacy of Harvie M. Conn," 214.
42 Conn, *A Clarified Vision for Urban Mission*, 217-218.
43 Keller, *Loving the City*, 104-105.
44 Keller, "Westminster - In Memory of Dr. Harvie Conn."
45 Keller, *Loving the City*, 106, 46; Tim Keller, *Center Church: Doing Balanced, Gospel-Centered Ministry in Your City* (Zondervan, 2012), 10; Tim Keller, *Gospel in Life Study Guide: Grace Changes Everything* (Zondervan, 2013), 127; Tim Keller, Jan 7, 2001, "Lord of the City," *The Tim Keller Sermon Archive*.

and rule the earth, as an "urban mandate."[46] Perhaps, most important for political purposes, Keller also deeply imbibed Conn's awareness of "systemic injustice" and the themes surrounding his proposed Christian solution.[47]

Like most leaders of the early evangelical left, Keller's main critique of Marxism was its materialism, not its moral claims. Karl Marx's solutions were incorrect because he grounded them in atheism and ignored the reality of human sin.[48] However, despite these major flaws, Keller believed Marxist hearts were in the right place. He stated in a sermon at Redeemer:

> The people I read who were the disciples of Marx were not villains. They were not fools. They cared about people . . . there are vast populations, millions of people, who have been in absolute serfdom and peasantry and poverty for years and years, and there's no way they're going to get out. There's no upward mobility. See, the people who read Marx said, 'We have to do something about this.' They weren't fools.[49]

Keller also singled Karl Marx out as the only "major thinker," other than God Himself, who "held up the common worker" with a high view of labor.[50] Unfortunately, for Marx and New Left thinkers downstream, like Ronald Dworkin, R. D. Laing, and Jean-Paul Sartre, their moral claims could not be justified apart from the moral foundation Christianity provided which had a "basis" for racial, social, and international justice.[51] Like progressive evangelicals before him, Keller addressed this problem by combining aspects of New Left thinking with Christianity.

---

46 Keller, *Loving the City,* 148, 134.
47 Keller, *Generous Justice,* 189.
48 Keller, February 16, 1997, "With a Religious Crowd," *The Tim Keller Sermon Archive;* Keller, October 22, 2000, "Made For Stewardship," *The Tim Keller Sermon Archive;* Keller, July, 15, 2001, "Arguing About Politics," *The Tim Keller Sermon Archive.*
49 Keller, "With a Religious Crowd."
50 Keller, "Made for Stewardship."
51 Keller, *The Reason for God,* 151-152; Keller, May 31, 1992, "Problem of Meaning; Is There Any Reason for Existence?," *The Tim Keller Sermon Archive;* Keller, "Center Church," 129; Keller, December 10, 2000, "Genesis—The Gospel According to God," *The Tim Keller Sermon Archive.*

From Keller's perspective, economics was a zero sum game. Impoverished children suffered because of an "inequitable distribution" of "goods and opportunities," not just a lack of them. Therefore, Christians who failed to share with the needy, were not only displaying "stinginess," but "injustice" itself. For believers, this kind of work, unlike "charity," was not optional. In fact, failing to share with the poor was tantamount to robbery because justice involved giving people their "rights" which included things like "access to opportunities," "financial resources," "access to education, legal assistance, [and] investment in job opportunities." The principle of "private property," however, was not an "absolute" right.[52]

In 2010, Keller told *Christianity Today*, "It's biblical that we owe the poor as much of our money as we can possibly give away." Using the language of moral obligation, he implied that the "havenots," on the basis of their need, possessed a legitimate claim to resources not distributed to them which belonged to the "haves." The church's job was to address these inequities by not only meeting needs, but also addressing "the conditions and social structures" that led to such needs in the first place. Keller pointed to liberation theologian Gustavo Gutiérrez's teaching on God's preference for the poor, and progressive evangelical John Perkins' teaching on "redistribution" as positive examples. He encouraged churches to get involved in "direct relief, individual development, community development, racial reconciliation, and social reform" which challenged and changed "social systems."[53]

In Keller's model, the gospel itself became the basis for Christians to do this "restorative and redistributive justice."[54] It was both a response to the gospel, and a means by which believers attracted unbelievers to Christianity.

---

52 Tim Keller [@timkellernyc], 2018, "The Bible's vision for interdependent community, in which private property is important but not an absolute, does not give a full support to any conventional political-economic agenda. It sits in critical judgment on them all.," Twitter, November 8, 2018, 11:26 a.m.

53 Keller, Generous Justice, 15, 92, 3, 115, 16-17, 125-126, 7, 117, 130-133; Tim Keller, "Tim Keller's Generous Justice," interview by Kristen Scharold, December 6, 2010, https://www.christianitytoday.com/ct/2010/december/10.69.html.

54 Keller, *The Reason for God*, 225.

According to Keller, this was not a new development either. He translated some Old Testament passages using the term "social justice" in the place of words that, in other translations, simply conveyed "righteousness" or "justice." God, in Keller's mind, charged Old Testament Israel to "create a culture of social justice." The application of this command, in the Mosaic law, was designed to reduce "unjust" economic disparities between social groups. According to "the prophets," "great disparities" resulted, at least in part, from a "selfish individualism" overcoming "concern for the common good."[55] In contrast, Jesus almost sounded like a "social justice radical activist" when He instructed selling possessions and giving to the poor in the Sermon on the Mount.[56] Christians who understood God's grace the best, were the "most sensitive to the social inequities," and churches who were true to the gospel were "just as involved in social justice issues as in bringing people to radical conversion."[57]

Keller's analysis for helping Christians battle disparities went deeper than just economic factors. Power relationships were also unequal. In His suffering, Jesus identified not only with the "poor," but also the "marginalized" and "oppressed."[58] The "substitutionary atonement" involved Jesus losing His "power" which, in turn, inspired Christians to be "radical agent[s] for social change" by giving up theirs.[59] The people of God were commanded to "administer true justice" to "groups [which] had no social power," which in modern times Keller expanded to include refugees, migrant workers, homeless, many single parents, and the elderly.[60] Much of his sermons on power relationships incorporated the teachings of Michel Foucault, who, according to Keller, was a "postmodern theorist," "socialist," and "French deconstructionist."[61]

55 Keller, *Generous Justice*, 356-366, 139, 9, 33-34.
56 Keller, May 9, 1999, "The Mount, Life in the Kingdom," *The Tim Keller Sermon Archive*.
57 Keller, *Generous Justice*, xxiv; Keller, November 9, 2003, "A Woman, A Slave, and a Gentile," *The Tim Keller Sermon Archive*.
58 Keller, *Reason for God*, 195-196.
59 Keller, March 11 2007, "Jesus and Politics," *The Tim Keller Sermon Archive*.
60 Keller, *Generous Justice*, 4.
61 Keller, October 5, 2003, "The Meaning of the City," *The Tim Keller Sermon Archive*; Keller, "Arguing About Politics;" October 10, 1993, "The Search for Identity," *The Tim Keller Sermon Archive*.

Keller stated that "the problem with the world" was "the way we use the truth" for the purpose of getting "power over other people." He thought Foucault was not only "right," but put it better than anyone else when he said, "Truth is a thing of this world: it is produced only by virtue of multiple forms of constraint. And it induces regular effects of power. Each society has its regime of truth, its 'general politics' of truth: that is, the types of discourse which it accepts . . . the means by which each is sanctioned . . . the status of those who are charged with saying what counts as true." Keller summarized Foucault's theory by stating, "truth is a thing of this world, and every person who claims to have the truth is really basically doing a power play."[62] He even quoted Jesus as stating, "Truth claims, in general, . . . are power plays"[63] in reaction to the Pharisees who were guilty of using "the Bible to get the right places in society, the high status, and to keep people down."[64] Keller, along with "postmodern thinkers," saw the "connection between truth and power" everywhere from discriminatory hiring practices to media narratives.[65]

In fact, from the Beatitudes, Keller believed Jesus taught that the quest for "power, success, comfort, and recognition" dominated the "kingdom of this world."[66] It even inescapably defined individuals themselves. New Left thinkers, like Foucault, saw in Hegel's concept of the "Other," a substitute for the alienation which took place at the Fall. Identity was not organically inherited or part of the fabric of duty and design, but rather, created through struggle against the "Other," which represented a negative, usually social standard.[67] Keller stated, in reliance on Foucault, that when "we form an identity . . . we get a sense of self-worth by despising the people who don't have it" which is the

---

62 Keller, "The Meaning of the City."
63 Keller, October 8, 2006; "Absolutism: Don't We All Have to Find Truth for Ourselves?," *The Tim Keller Sermon Archive.*
64 Keller, May 16, 2010, "Integrity," *The Tim Keller Sermon Archive.*
65 Keller, March 3, 2002, "Passionate Grace," *The Tim Keller Sermon Archive.*
66 Keller, "Arguing About Politics."
67 Roger Scruton, *Fools, Frauds and Firebrands: Thinkers of the New Left* (Bloomsbury Publishing, 2015), 74-76.

same as bolstering "a self through exclusion of the 'Other.'" Simply put, people use their chosen identities, based on things like their work, religion, and political affiliation, to exert power by vilifying others who are "not like them." Only in Christianity did Keller see "a basis" for "accepting" different people.

No revolution could escape the reality of power except "the Kingdom of God," ruled by a "king without a quarter," "power," or "recognition," and requiring his followers to give up their power as well.[68] Keller saw Christianity as "a kind of truth" which empowered and liberated its believers to "serve and love others, not control them."[69] He agreed with liberation theologian James Cone that slaves, because of their "experience of oppression," were able "to see things in the Bible" like a "God who comes down from heaven and becomes a poor human being," which "many of their masters were blind to." This difference in experience was so great it nurtured a "real Christianity" as opposed to the oppressive "Master's religion."[70] Real Christianity was the escape hatch from the view that truth "inevitably leads to power," as it not only addressed economic disparities, but also unequal power relationships.[71] Therefore, the "church" could not ally or align itself with the "secular left or right" for the sake of "political power," without giving up its "spiritual power and credibility with nonbelievers."[72] Christians needed a different political approach.

Because Christianity, in Keller's view, grounded both personal ethics and social justice in a transcendent standard, it represented an unconventional political perspective outside of earthly political parties. Keller conceived of "liberal politics" as a philosophy dedicated to doing "whatever you want with your body but not whatever you want with your money." Their

---

68 Keller, "Arguing About Politics."
69 Keller, "Passionate Grace."
70 Keller, May 31, 2000, "What is Freedom" *The Tim Keller Sermon Archive*; Keller, May, 3, 1998, "My God is a Rock; Listening to the African-American Spirituals," *The Tim Keller Sermon Archive*.
71 Keller, "Passionate Grace."
72 Tim Keller, Forward to *In Search of the Common Good: Christian Fidelity in a Fractured World* (InterVarsity Press, 2019), 3.

concern was "economic justice" in "taking care of the poor."[73] Throughout his ministry Keller identified "social justice" concern with more politically progressive groups.[74] On the other hand, "conservatives," he told his congregation, wanted "legislation that supports the family" and "traditional values, but when it comes to giving money to the poor, that should be voluntary." Liberals wanted to legislate "social morality" but not "personal morality" and conservatives wanted to legislate "personal morality" but not "social morality."[75] Neither represented an acceptable Christian position.

The problem with closely aligning with either political philosophy, according to Keller, was that they could easily culturally "colonize" Christians into versions of "extreme individualism." The sexual rights of "blue state" individualism and the property rights of "red state" individualism were comparable to false religions coopting Christians into their mold.[76] Blue evangelicals were "quiet about the biblical teaching" on "abortion, sexuality, and gender." Red evangelicals were "silent" when "political allies fan[ned] the flames of racial resentment toward immigrants." Keller wrote that "Theologically, both political pols are suspect, because one makes an idol out of individual freedom, and the other makes an idol out of race and nation, blood and soil. In both something created and earthly is deified."[77]Alternatively, Keller proposed a third option in the "biblical worldview."[78]

While Christians could "vote across a spectrum" for practical reasons, they should also "feel somewhat uncomfortable in either political party."[79]

73 Keller, March 25, 1990, "Goodness, Faithfulness," *The Tim Keller Sermon Archive*.
74 Keller, April 24, 2005, "The Community of Grace," *The Tim Keller Sermon Archive*; Keller, March 19, 2006, "The Openness of the Kingdom." *The Tim Keller Sermon Archive*.
75 Keller, "Goodness, Faithfulness."
76 "Tim Keller on Changing the Culture Without Being Colonized by It," (The Gospel Coalition, 2019), https://www.youtube.com/watch?time_continue=4&v=eDqJkfhTu RY&feature=emb_title.
77 Tim Keller, Forward to *In Search of the Common Good: Christian Fidelity in a Fractured World*.
78 "Tim Keller on Changing the Culture Without Being Colonized by It."
79 Keller, "Arguing About Politics;" "You Need to Hear Tim Keller's Takedown of Radical Nationalism," *Relevant Magazine* (blog), December 10, 2018, https://relevantmagazine.com/current/you-need-to-hear-tim-kellers-takedown-of-radical-nationalism.

The Bible deconstructed "all secular understandings of economics" including "capitalism [which] uses the engine of individuals envying individuals, and communism or socialism [which] just uses the engine of classes envying classes."[80] In order to be biblical, Keller thought consistent Christians would, in applying an understanding of justice and equality, "sometimes . . . side with one school of thought, [and] other times they will side with another" because secular theories of justice addressed certain "facets of biblical justice" without addressing them all.[81] The biblical idea, that "the community has some claim on" private "profits and assets," but that those items should not be "confiscated," did "not fit well with either a capitalist or a socialist economy."[82] Instead, Christians needed to, on some level, politically operate outside the available political parties. This, of course, meant spending more effort distancing themselves from Republicans, whom evangelicals had traditionally supported, than it did Democrats.

In 2017, Keller signed a statement, along with other more progressive leaning evangelicals like Richard Mouw and Ed Stetzer, urging "President Trump to Reconsider Reduction in Refugee Resettlement."[83] The next year Keller, along with "50 evangelical Christian leaders," including Jim Wallis, gathered at Wheaton College to discuss their concern that evangelicalism had "become too closely associated with President Trump's polarizing politics."[84] In 2020, Keller briefly joined the elder board of the AND Campaign, led by Michael Wear, one of President Obama's former faith advisors, and Justin Giboney, a Democrat political strategist. The campaign produced a "2020 Presidential Election Statement"

80 Keller, "Arguing About Politics;" Keller, September 27, 1998, "When All You've Ever Wanted Isn't Enough," *The Tim Keller Sermon Archive.*
81 Keller, Generous Justice, 159; Tim Keller, "A Biblical Critique of Secular Justice and Critical Theory," *Life in the Gospel,* July 31, 2020, https://quarterly.gospelinlife.com/a-biblical-critique-of-secular-justice-and-critical-theory.
82 Keller, A Biblical Critique of Secular Justice and Critical Theory."
83 "Evangelical Leaders from All 50 States Urge President Trump to Reconsider Reduction in Refugee Resettlement," *The Washington Post,* February 3, 2017, sec. A18.
84 Emily McFarlan Miller, "Evangelical Leaders Gather at Wheaton to Discuss Future of the Movement in Trump Era," *Sojourners,* April 17, 2018, https://sojo.net/articles/evangelical-leaders-gather-wheaton-discuss-future-movement-trump-era.

to "promote social justice and moral order" which included concern for "racial disparities," support for the "Fairness for All Act," "comprehensive immigration reform," and "affordable health care," while discouraging abortion.[85]

Keller's political vision was perhaps most clearly articulated in his 2008 book, *Reason for God*, in which he signaled his hope that "younger Christians . . . could make the older form of culture wars obsolete" through their version of Christianity which is "much more concerned about the poor and social justice than Republicans have been, and at the same time much more concerned about upholding classic Christian moral and sexual ethics than Democrats have been."[86] Christianity offered an "identity" which prioritized service "instead of power."[87] A "new human society, a new human order, [and] a new set of social arrangements not based on power and pride" was on the horizon in what the Bible called "the lofty city."[88] The vision of Redeemer Presbyterian was "to help build a great city for all people through a movement of the gospel that brings personal conversion, community formation, social justice, and cultural renewal to New York City and, through it, the world."[89] Keller said, "The whole purpose of salvation is to cleanse and purify this material world."[90]

Some have tried to analyze Tim Keller's social justice position as a subset of concerns stemming from his crafting "new lines of thought" for communicating with "postmoderns."[91] Michel Foucault was not the only postmodern New Left thinker Keller gleaned from in his ministry. For example, in crafting his New City Catechism, created to meet the challenges of a postmodern

85 "AND Campaign," AND Campaign, accessed May 1, 2020, https://andcampaign.org
86 Keller, *Reason for God*, xix-xx.
87 Keller, February 25, 2001, "Born into Community," *The Tim Keller Sermon Archive.*
88 Keller, May 1, 2005, "The City of God," *The Tim Keller Sermon Archive.*
89 Keller, September 18, 2005, "Christ, Our Life," *The Tim Keller Sermon Archive.*
90 Tim Keller, "Cultural Renewal: The Role of the Intrapreneur and the Entrepreneur" (Entrepreneurship Forum, Lamb's Ballroom, Times Square, March 25, 2006), 4:30, 9. https://web.archive.org/web/20060622051746/http://www.faithandwork.org/uploads/photos/461-1%20Cultural%20Renewal_%20The%20Role%20of%20th.mp3.
91 Ian Campbell and William Schweitzer, *Engaging with Keller: Thinking Through the Theology of an Influential Evangelical* (EP Books, 2013), 9, 21.

world, Keller partially relied on understandings gleaned from Charles Taylor's "buffered self narrative."[92] Keller also taught his congregation that Martin Heidegger's theory of "alienation" paralleled Jesus' teaching in the story of the Prodigal Son.[93] In 2018, he helped launch the "Living Out Church Audit," designed to help churches be inclusive toward "LGBTQ+/same-sex attracted" individuals.[94] Because of Keller's non-traditional conceptions of sin, hell, the Trinity, the church's mission, biblical interpretation, creation, and ecclesiology, a group of traditional Presbyterians wrote *Engaging Keller,* in 2013. However, there is another way to understand Keller's left-leaning tendency.

From his earliest and most formative years as a Christian and theologian, Keller, who already stood politically with progressives, was influenced by the evangelical left. Tom Skinner, Elward Ellis, Harvie Conn, Richard Mouw, and John Perkins all contributed to helping Keller integrate his faith with his politics. Keller often interpreted Scriptures concerning politics and econom-ics in ways consistent with neo-Kuyperian and liberation theologies. Keller then successfully marketed his ideas to the evangelical world. Today, having stepped down from pastoring at Redeemer Presbyterian in 2017, Tim Keller teaches for Reformed Theological Seminary and works with Redeemer's City to City church planting network, where he continues to spread his ideas on "contextualization" which he first learned from Harvie Conn. Keller's contri-bution to moving evangelicals in a leftward direction cannot be underesti-mated. The impact of his teachings will be felt for years to come.

---

92 Tim Keller, "Catechesis for a Secular Age," interview by James K.A. Smith, September 1, 2017, https://www.cardus.ca/comment/article/catechesis-for-a-secular-age.
93 Keller, November 2, 2008, "We Had to Celebrate," *The Tim Keller Sermon Archive.*
94 "The Living Out Church Audit," Living Out, accessed August 21, 2020, https://www.livingout.org/resources/the-living-out-church-audit.

BIBLIOGRAPHY

Yale Center for Faith and Culture. "'A Common Word' Christian Response." Accessed May 1, 2020. https://faith.yale.edu/common-word/common-word-christian-response.

Russell Moore. "A Conversation with Ronald J. Sider," August 21, 2019. https://www.russellmoore.com/2019/08/21/a-conversation-with-ronald-j-sider.

Change.org. "A Declaration by American Evangelicals Concerning Donald Trump," 2016. https://www.change.org/p/donald-trump-a-declaration-by-american-evangelicals-concerning-donald-trump.

"A Response to the International Congress on World Evangelization." *Sojourners*, November 1, 1974. https://sojo.net/magazine/november-1974/response-international-congress-world-evangelization.

"A Word from Frederick Douglas." *Right On*, March 1972.

Evangelical Immigration Table. "About." Accessed May 1, 2020. http://evangelicalimmigrationtable.com/about.

Adriel, Rose. "For Those With Ears to Hear: A Review of 'The Color of Compromise.'" Evangelicals for Social Action, March 13, 2019. https://www.evangelicalsforsocialaction.org/resources/book-reviews/ears-hear-review-color-compromise.

Alexander, Fred. "Integration Now," December 1965.

———. "White Pastor, Black Church." *Freedom Now*, December 1969.

Alexander, John. *Being Church: Reflections on How to Live as the People of God.* Wipf and Stock Publishers, 2012.

———. "Madison Avenue Jesus." *Sojourners*, September 1, 1971. https://sojo.net/magazine/fall-1971/madison-avenue-jesus.

Allison, Tom. "Beck Distorts Wallis' Comments to Claim He Is a 'Marxist.'" Media Matters for America, March 24, 2010. https://www.mediamatters.org/glenn-beck/beck-distorts-wallis-comments-claim-he-marxist.

Alsdurf, Phyllis. "Evangelical Feminists: Ministry Is the Issue." *Christianity Today*, July 21, 1978.

Amerson, Philip. "Excess or Access?" *Sojourners*, July 1, 1979. https://sojo.net/magazine/july-1979/excess-or-access.

AND Campaign. "AND Campaign." Accessed May 1, 2020. https://andcampaign.org.

Ashford, Bruce, and Chris Pappalardo. *One Nation Under God: A Christian Hope for American Politics.* B&H Publishing Group, 2015.

Balmer, Randall. *Encyclopedia of Evangelicalism.* Westminster John Knox Press, 2002.

Bebbington, David. *Evangelicalism in Modern Britain: A History from the 1730s to the 1980s.* Routledge, 2003.

Becker, Amy Julia. "Why I Am Ditching the Label 'Evangelical' in the Trump Era." *Washington Post*, October 18, 2017. https://www.washingtonpost.com/news/acts-of-faith/wp/2017/10/18/why-i-am-ditching-the-label-evangelical-in-the-trump-era.

Beebe, Ralph. "Voice of Calvary Has the Sound of a Friend." *Evangelical Friend*, November 1979. https://digitalcommons.georgefox.edu/cgi/viewcontent.cgi?referer=https://www.bing.com/&httpsredir=1&article=1131&context=nwym_evangelical_friend.

Bender, Harold. "Anabaptist Theology of Discipleship," *The Mennonite Quarterly Review 24*, no.1, (1950).

———. "The Anabaptist Vision." *Church History 13*, no. 1 (1944): 3-24. Accessed July 2, 2020. www.jstor.org/stable/3161001.

Berg, David. "Our Declaration of Revolution." The xFamily.org Publications Database, September 1968. https://pubs.xfamily.org/text.php?t=1336.

Lausanne Movement. "Billy Graham and John Stott." Accessed March 13, 2020. https://www.lausanne.org/billy-graham-and-john-stott.

Blair, Leonardo. "JD Greear Endorses Black Lives Matter as Gospel Issue, Denounces Organization." *The Christian Post*, June 10, 2020. https://www.christianpost.com/news/jd-greear-endorses-black-lives-matter-as-gospel-issue-denounces-blm-organization.html.

Blair, Ralph. *An Evangelical Look at Homosexuality.* Homosexual Community Counseling Center, 1972.

Blake, John. "Progressive Preacher: As an Activist, Evangelical Christian, Jim Wallis Challenges Religious Right." *Atlanta Journal-Constitution*, May 21, 2005.

Boldrey, Dick. "Technocracy and Women's Liberation." *Sojourners*, June 1, 1972. https://sojo.net/magazine/summer-1972/technocracy-and-womens-liberation.

"Book Briefs: July 29, 1977." *Christianity Today*, July 29, 1977.

"Books of the Century." *Christianity Today*, April 24, 2000.

Brown, Dale. "Revolutionary Implications of the Atonement." *Sojourners*, May 1, 1973. https://sojo.net/magazine/may-june-1973/ revolutionary-implications-atonement.

————. "The Crucified God by Jurgen Moltmann." *Sojourners*, August 1, 1975. https://sojo.net/magazine/august-september-1975/ crucified-god-jurgen-moltmann.

————. "Thy Kingdom Come." *Sojourners*, June 1, 1974. https://sojo.net/ magazine/june-july-1974/thy-kingdom-come.

————. "'We Have Seen the Enemy . . . And They Is Us.'" *Sojourners*, April 1, 1975. https://sojo.net/magazine/april-1975/we-have-seen-enemyand-they-us.

Brownson, James. Bible, Gender, *Sexuality: Reframing the Church's Debate on Same-Sex Relationships.* Wm. B. Eerdmans Publishing, 2013.

Burkholder, John. "Money." *Sojourners*, December 1, 1974. https://sojo.net/ magazine/december-1974/money.

Burkholder, Jared, and David Cramer. *The Activist Impulse: Essays on the Intersection of Evangelicalism and Anabaptism.* Wipf and Stock Publishers, 2012.

CBE International. "CBE's Mission and Values." Accessed March 12, 2020. https://www.cbeinternational.org/content/cbes-mission.

Evangelicals for Social Action. "Chicago Declaration of Evangelical Social Concern," November 2, 2012. https:// www.evangelicalsforsocialaction.org/about-esa-2/history/ chicago-declaration-evangelical-social-concern.

"Choice Evangelical Books of 1970." *Christianity Today*, February 26, 1971. https:// www.christianitytoday.com/ct/1971/february-26/choice-evangelical-books-of-1970.html.

"Christians for Biblical Equality President to Teach Class on Gender Equality and Christianity." PRWeb. January 31, 2016. https://www.prweb.com/releases/2016/01/prweb13191511.htm.

Clark, Fred. "Rich Christians in an Age of Hunger." Patheos (blog), December 21, 2005. https://www.patheos.com/blogs/slacktivist/2005/12/21/rich-christians-in-an-age-of-hunger.

Cone, James. *The Cross and the Lynching Tree.* Orbis Books, 2011.

Crable, Ad. "Arthur Gish, County Native, Global Activist Dies." *Lancaster Online*, August 9, 2010. https://web.archive.org/web/20100809235820/http://articles.lancasteronline.com/local/4/271775.

David Berg. "Creating a New Society." Accessed February 19, 2020. https://www.davidberg.org/mission/a-sample-community-deep-in-the-heart-of-texas.

Crowther, Edward. *Southern Evangelicals and the Coming of the Civil War. Studies in American Religion.* E. Mellen Press, 2000.

"David P. Gushee." Accessed March 12, 2020. http://www.davidpgushee.com/davidpgushee.

Davids, Peter. "God and Mammon In the Early Church." *Sojourners*, March 1, 1978. https://sojo.net/magazine/march-1978/god-and-mammon-early-church.

———. "The People of God and the Wealth of the People." *Sojourners*, June 1, 1975. https://sojo.net/magazine/june-july-1975/people-god-and-wealth-people.

Day, Dorothy. "Catholic Worker Movement." *The Catholic Worker*, May 1936.

———. https://www.catholicworker.org/dorothyday/articles/300.html.

Dayton, Donald. *Discovering an Evangelical Heritage.* Harper & Row, 1976.

————. "Recovering a Heritage, Part III: The Lane Rebellion and the Founding of Oberlin College." *Sojourners,* October 1, 1974. https://sojo.net/magazine/october-1974/recovering-heritage.

————. "Recovering a Heritage, Part IV: The 'Christian Radicalism' of Oberlin College." *Sojourners,* November 1, 1974. https://sojo.net/magazine/november-1974/recovering-heritage.

————. "Recovering a Heritage, Part V: The Rescue Case." *Sojourners,* December 1, 1974. https://sojo.net/magazine/december-1974/recovering-heritage.

————. "Recovering a Heritage, Part VI: Orange Scott and the Wesleyan Methodist." *Sojourners,* January 1, 1975. https://sojo.net/magazine/january-1975/recovering-heritage.

————. "Recovering a Heritage, Part VII: The Sermons of Luther Lee." *Sojourners,* February 1, 1975. https://sojo.net/magazine/february-1975/recovering-heritage.

Dayton, Donald W., and Lucille Sider Dayton. "Recovering a Heritage, Part II: Evangelical Feminism, by Donald W. Dayton and Lucille Sider Dayton." *Sojourners,* August 1, 1974. https://sojo.net/magazine/august-september-1974/recovering-heritage.

Dayton, Lucille Sider. "The Feminist Movement and Scripture." *Sojourners,* August 1, 1974. https://sojo.net/magazine/august-september-1974/feminist-movement-and-scripture.

Dayton, Lucille Sider, and Donald W. Dayton. "Women in the Holiness Movement," May 1, 1974. https://resources.wesleyan.org/wp-content/uploads/Dayton-Donald-Wilber-Lucille-Sider-Women-in-the-Holiness-Movement.pdf.

Dever, Mark. "How to Kill a Church." *Desiring God,* October 9, 2017. https://www.desiringgod.org/messages/gospel-purity/excerpts/how-to-kill-a-church.

Diamond, Sara. *Right-Wing Movements in the United States,* 1945-1992 (University of California, Berkeley, 1993).

Dochuk, Darren, Thomas S. Kidd, and Kurt W. Peterson, eds. *American Evangelicalism: George Marsden and the State of American Religious History.* Notre Dame, Indiana: University of Notre Dame Press, 2014.

Douglas, James Dixon. *Let the Earth Hear His Voice.* World Wide Publications, 1975.

Doyle, Barrie. "The Religious Campaign: Backing Their Man." Christianity Today, October 27, 1972. *Sojourners.* "Ed Stetzer," September 1, 2013. https://sojo.net/biography/ed-stetzer.

Ediger, Peter. "Explo '72." *Sojourners,* September 1, 1972. https://sojo.net/magazine/fall-1972/explo-72.

―――. "Signs of a New Order." *Sojourners,* March 1, 1973. https://sojo.net/magazine/march-april-1973/signs-new-order.

―――. "The War Crimes Committee." *Right On,* May 1, 1971.

Edwards, Jonathan. *The Works of President Edwards.* v. 4. New York: Leavitte, Trow & Co., 1844.

Eells, Robert, and Bartell Nyberg. *Lonely Walk: The Life of Senator Mark Hatfield.* Christian Herald Books, 1979.

Wipf and Stock Publishers. "Endorsements and Reviews." Accessed April 22, 2020. https://wipfandstock.com/the-chicago-declaration.html.

The Ethics & Religious Liberty Commission of the Southern Baptist Convention. "ERLC: About." Accessed March 11, 2020. https://erlc.com/about.

Escobar, Samuel. *Liberation Theology and the Development of Latin American Evangelical Theology.* Wheaton College, 2011. https://youtu.be/EP35aHIZvYo.

Eskridge, Larry. *God's Forever Family: The Jesus People Movement in America.* OUP USA, 2013.

"Eutychus and His Kin: August 16, 1974." *Christianity Today,* August 16, 1974.

"Eutychus and His Kin: January 17, 1975." *Christianity Today,* January 17, 1975. https://www.christianitytoday.com/ct/1975/january-17/eutychus-and-his-kin.html.

"Evangelical Leaders from All 50 States Urge President Trump to Reconsider Reduction in Refugee Resettlement." *The Washington Post,* February 3, 2017, sec. A18.

"Evangelicals on Justice: Socially Speaking . . . " *Christianity Today,* December 21, 1973.

Fager, Charles. "Ethics, Principalities and Nonviolence." *Sojourners,* November 1, 1974. https://sojo.net/magazine/november-1974/ethics-principalities-and-nonviolence.

Fea, John. *Believe Me: The Evangelical Road to Donald Trump.* Wm. B. Eerdmans Publishing. 2018.

———. "Ron Sider: I'm Still an 'Evangelical.'" *The Way of Improvement Leads Home* (blog). January 17, 2020. https://thewayofimprovement.com/2020/01/17/ron-sider-im-still-an-evangelical.

Finger, Thomas. "Christians and Marxists." *Sojourners*, April 1, 1977. https://sojo.net/magazine/april-1977/christians-and-marxists.

Finger, Tom. "Reformed/Anabaptist Conversation: Jesus as Ethical Norm." *Sojourners*, December 1, 1976. https://sojo.net/magazine/december-1976/reformedanabaptist-conversation-jesus-ethical-norm.

Finnerty, Adam. "The Christian Model." *Sojourners*, May 1, 1974. https://sojo.net/magazine/may-1974/christian-model.

Finstuen, Andrew, Anne Wills, and Grant Wacker. *Billy Graham: American Pilgrim.* Oxford Studies in Western Esotericism. Oxford University Press, 2017.

Fiske, Edward. "The Closest Thing To A White House Chaplain." *The New York Times*, June 8, 1969. https://archive.nytimes.com/www.nytimes.com/books/97/07/06/reviews/graham-magazine.html.

FitzGerald, Francis. *The Evangelicals: The Struggle to Shape America.* Simon & Schuster, 2017.

Forbes, Cheryl. "Survey Results: Changing Church Roles for Women?" *Christianity Today*, September 27, 1974.

Forest, Jim. "There Was Always Bread." *Sojourners*, December 1, 1976. https://sojo.net/magazine/december-1976/there-was-always-bread.

Formicola, Jo Renee, and Hubert Morken, eds. *Religious Leaders and Faith-Based Politics: Ten Profiles.* Lanham, MD: Rowman & Littlefield Publishers, 2001.

Fuller Theological Seminary. "Catalog: School of Theology and School of World Mission, Academic Year 1970-1972." Academic Catalogs, 1970. https://digitalcommons.fuller.edu/academic_catalogs/12.

Gallagher, Sharon. "From Right On! To Radix: A Short History." *Radix*, August 1979.

———. "Ode to Caesar." *Sojourners*, March 1, 1976. https://sojo.net/magazine/march-1976/ode-caesar.

———. "Woman vs. Politics in Mexico City." *Right On*, September 1975.

Gasaway, Brantley. *Progressive Evangelicals and the Pursuit of Social Justice.* University of North Carolina Press, 2014.

Gay, Craig. *With Liberty and Justice for Whom?: The Recent Evangelical Debate Over Capitalism.* W.B. Eerdmans Publishing Company, 1991.

Genovese, Eugene. *The Southern Front: History and Politics in the Cultural War.* University of Missouri Press, 1995.

Gilbreath, Edward. "A Prophet Out of Harlem." *Christianity Today*, September 16, 1996.

———. "Thomas Skinner: A Prophet out of Harlem." *Christianity Today*, September 16, 1996. https://www.christianitytoday.com/ct/1996/september16/6ta036.html.

Gilgoff, Dan. "Evangelical Minister Jim Wallis Is in Demand in Obama's Washington." *US News & World Report*, March 31, 2009. https://www.usnews.com/news/religion/articles/2009/03/31/evangelical-minister-jim-wallis-is-in-demand-in-obamas-washington.

Gill, David. "Toward a Radical Christian Identity." *Right On*, October 1974.

Gish, Art. *Living in Christian Community.* Herald Press, 1979.

———. *The New Left and Christian Radicalism.* Eerdmans, 1970.

———. "Reconsideration." *Sojourners*, June 1, 1972.

————. "The New Left and Christian Radicalism." *Sojourners*, September 1, 1971. https://sojo.net/magazine/fall-1971/new-left-and-christian-radicalism.

Goodstein, Laurie. "Without a Pastor of His Own, Obama Turns to Five." *The New York Times*, March 14, 2009, sec. U.S. https://www.nytimes.com/2009/03/15/us/politics/15pastor.html.

Granberg-Michaelson, Wes. "Liberating the Church." *Sojourners*, September 1, 1976. https://sojo.net/magazine/september-1976/liberating-church.

————. "No King But Caesar." *Sojourners*, January 1, 1976. https://sojo.net/magazine/january-1976/no-king-caesar.

————. "Politics and Spirituality." *Sojourners*, April 1, 1974. https://sojo.net/magazine/april-1974/politics-and-spirituality.

————. "Suffering with the Victims." *Sojourners*, July 1, 1976. https://sojo.net/magazine/july-august-1976/suffering-victims.

————. *Unexpected Destinations: An Evangelical Pilgrimage to World Christianity*. Eerdmans Publishing Company, 2011.

Guinan, Ed. "In Communion with Trampled Bodies." *Sojourners*, April 1, 1975. https://sojo.net/magazine/april-1975/communion-trampled-bodies.

Gushee, David. Interview with David P. Gushee, author of *Still Christian: Following Jesus Out of American Evangelicalism*. Reading Religion. Accessed March 12, 2020. http://readingreligion.org/content/interview-david-p-gushee-author-still-christian-following-jesus-out-american-evangelicalism.

Gutiérrez, Gustavo. *A Theology of Liberation: History, Politics, and Salvation*. Orbis Books, 1973.

Hall, Matthew. "Right now Ron Sider is dropping pro-life bombs all over #EFL2016. If you are pro-life, you need to listen humbly," Twitter, January 26, 2016, 10:44 p.m., https://twitter.com/MatthewJHall/status/690198283034181632

Halaschak, Zachary. "'This Is Not a Political Issue': Joel Osteen Says Floyd Death 'Ignited Something in Me.'" *Washington Examiner,* June 10, 2020. https://www.washingtonexaminer.com/news/this-is-not-a-political-issue-joel-osteen-says-floyd-death-ignited-something-in-me.

Harrold, Stanley. *The Abolitionists and the South,* 1831-1861. University Press of Kentucky, 2015.

Hart, Darryl. *From Billy Graham to Sarah Palin: Evangelicals and the Betrayal of American Conservatism.* Eerdmans Publishing Company, 2011.

Hatfield, Mark. *Between a Rock and a Hard Place.* Pocket Books, 1977.

———. "Mark Hatfield on World Hunger." *Right On,* March 1975.

———. "And Still They Hunger." *Sojourners,* January 1, 1975. https://sojo.net/magazine/january-1975/and-still-they-hunger.

———. "On Repentance and National Humiliation." *Sojourners,* April 1, 1974. https://sojo.net/magazine/april-1974/repentance-and-national-humiliation.

———. "Piety and Patriotism." *Sojourners,* May 1, 1973. https://sojo.net/magazine/may-june-1973/piety-and-patriotism.

———. "Repentance, Politics, and Power." *Sojourners,* January 1, 1974. https://sojo.net/magazine/january-1974/repentance-politics-and-power.

———. "The Prayer Breakfast." *Sojourners,* February 1, 1976. https://sojo.net/magazine/february-1976/prayer-breakfast.

————. *Conflict and Conscience.* Word Books, 1971.

Hearn, Virginia, ed. *Our Struggle to Serve: The Stories of 15 Evangelical Women.* Waco, Tex: Word Books, 1979.

Henry, Carl. *Confessions of a Theologian: An Autobiography.* Waco, Tex: Word Books, 1986.

————. "Decades of Gains and Losses." *Christianity Today,* March 12, 1976.

————. "Evangelical Renewal." *Christianity Today,* January 5, 1973.

————. "The Gospel and Society." *Christianity Today.* September 13, 1974

————. "Winds of Promise." *Christianity Today,* June 5, 1970.

————. *Evangelical Responsibility in Contemporary Theology.* Pathway Books. A Series of Contemporary Evangelical Studies. Eerdmans, 1957.

————. *The Uneasy Conscience of Modern Fundamentalism.* Eerdmans Publishing Company, 2003.

"Here We Stand: An Evangelical Declaration on Marriage." *Christianity Today,* June 26, 2015. https://www.christianitytoday.com/ct/2015/june-web-only/here-we-stand-evangelical-declaration-on-marriage.html.

Hillard, Clarence. "A Dissent to the Covenant Issued at the International Congress on World Evangelization." *Sojourners,* November 1, 1974. https://sojo.net/magazine/november-1974/dissent-covenant-issued-international-congress-world-evangelization.

Himes, Brant. *For a Better Worldliness: Abraham Kuyper, Dietrich Bonhoeffer, and Discipleship for the Common Good.* Wipf and Stock Publishers, 2018.

Hollyday, Joyce. "A Little History . . . " *Sojourners,* September 1, 1981. https://sojo.net/magazine/september-1981/little-history.

Hooser, Michael. *Let the Earth Hear His Voice*. World Wide Pictures, 1974. https://www.lausanne.org/content/documentary-about-1974-congress.

Horowitz, Daniel. *Betty Friedan and the Making of The Feminine Mystique: The American Left, the Cold War, and Modern Feminism*. University of Massachusetts Press, 2000.

Hunt, Keith, and Gladys Hunt. *For Christ and the University: The Story of InterVarsity Christian Fellowship of the USA - 1940-1990*. InterVarsity Press, 2009.

Hyer, Majorie. "Evangelicals: Tackling the Gut Issues." *Christian Century*, December 19, 1973.

Janzen, David. "The Empire of Mammon and the Joyous Fellowship." *Sojourners*, September 1, 1973. https://sojo.net/magazine/september-october-1973/empire-mammon-and-joyous-fellowship.Sojourners. "Jemar Tisby," July 2, 2018. https://sojo.net/biography/jemar-tisby.

Jenkins, Jack. "Mitt Romney Joins Evangelical Racial Justice March in DC." News & Reporting, June 7, 2020. https://www.christianitytoday.com/news/2020/june/mitt-romney-dc-march-thabiti-anyabwile-christians.html.

Johnson, Dale. "A Conversation With Frankie Schaeffer." *Right On*, July 8, 1974.

Johnson, Dana. "The New Left and Christian Radicalism." Review of Religious Research 13, no. 2 (1972): 153–54. https://doi.org/10.2307/3509752.

Kaleem, Jaweed. "Jim Wallis Talks Faith's Role In Politics, Gay Marriage And Immigration." HuffPost, April 5, 2013. https://www.huffpost.com/entry/jim-wallis-faith-politics-immigration_n_3024458.

Keller, Tim. *Cultural Engagement: Center Church, Part Five*. Zondervan, 2013.

————. "Cultural Renewal: The Role of the Intrapreneur and the Entrepreneur." Presented at the Entrepreneurship Forum, Lamb's Ballroom, Times Square, March 25, 2006. https://web.archive.org/web/20060622051746/ http://www.faithandwork.org/uploads/photos/461-1%20Cultural%20 Renewal_%20The%20Role%20of%20th.mp3.

————. *Every Good Endeavor: Connecting Your Work to God's Work.* Penguin Publishing Group, 2014.

————. *Generous Justice: How God's Grace Makes Us Just.* Penguin Publishing Group, 2012.

————. *Gospel in Life Study Guide: Grace Changes Everything.* Zondervan, 2013.

————. *The Reason for God: Belief in an Age of Skepticism.* Penguin Publishing Group, 2008.

Keller, Timothy, and John Inazu. *Uncommon Ground: Living Faithfully in a World of Difference.* Thomas Nelson, 2020.

Kirk, Andrew. "Marx and the Bible." *Sojourners,* January 1, 1977. https://sojo. net/magazine/january-1977/marx-and-bible.

Krapohl, Robert, and Charles Lippy. *The Evangelicals: A Historical, Thematic, and Biographical Guide.* Greenwood Publishing Group, 1999.

Kuyper, Abraham. *Common Grace: God's Gifts for a Fallen World,* Volume 1. Abraham Kuyper Collected Works in Public Theology. Faithlife Corporation, 2016.

————. *Calvinism: Six Stone-Lectures.* Höveker & Wormser, 1899.

Kyle, Richard. *Evangelicalism: An Americanized Christianity.* Taylor & Francis, 2017.

Lahr, Angela. *Millennial Dreams and Apocalyptic Nightmares: The Cold War Origins of Political Evangelicalism.* Oxford University Press, USA, 2007.

Lane, Bill. "Lessons from Vietnam." *Sojourners*, March 1, 1973. https://sojo.net/magazine/march-april-1973/lessons-vietnam.

———. "New Directions for the Church." *Sojourners*, January 1, 1973. https://sojo.net/magazine/january-february-1973/new-directions-church.

———. "The Christian Radical." *Sojourners*, October 1, 1974. https://sojo.net/magazine/october-1974/christian-radical.

Larson, Bruce. *Ask Me to Dance*. Words Books, 1972.

Larson, Roy. "Historic Workshop: Evangelicals Do U-Turn, Take on Social Problems." *Chicago Sun-Times*, December 1, 1973.

Leeman, Jonathan. "Week #10—What Christians Should Ask of Government: To Treat People Equally (Justice and Identity Politics)," 9 Marks, November 3, 2016, https://www.9marks.org/article/week-10-what-christians-should-ask-of-government-to-treat-people-equally-justice-and-identity-politics/#_ftnref2.

"Living with Rich Christians in an Age of Hunger." *American Society of Missiology*, 2019. https://www.youtube.com/watch?v=g85cwDBqhj0.

Loritts, Bryan. *Letters to a Birmingham Jail*. Moody Publishers, 2014.

Loudon, Tom. "If Christ Came Back Today." *Sojourners*, September 1, 1971. https://sojo.net/magazine/fall-1971/if-christ-came-back-today.

Lund, Compiled by Emily. "Trump Won. Here's How 20 Evangelical Leaders Feel." Christianity Today, November 11, 2016. https://www.christianity-today.com/ct/2016/november-web-only/trump-won-how-evangelical-leaders-feel.html.

MacDonald, Dennis. "Demythologizing the Present." *Sojourners*, March 1, 1973. https://sojo.net/magazine/march-april-1973/demythologizing-present.

————. "Prophetic Resistance." *Sojourners*, March 1, 1972. https://sojo.net/magazine/spring-1972/prophetic-resistance.

Manhattan Declaration. "Manhattan Declaration: A Call to Christian Conscience," November 20, 2009. https://www.manhattandeclaration.org.

Marsden, George. *Understanding Fundamentalism and Evangelicalism*. Eerdmans Publishing Company, 1991.

————. *Fundamentalism and American Culture*. Oxford University Press, 2006.

————. *Reforming Fundamentalism: Fuller Seminary and the New Evangelicalism*. W.B. Eerdmans, 1987.

Marsh, Charles. *The Beloved Community: How Faith Shapes Social Justice from the Civil Rights Movement to Today*. Basic Books, 2008.

Martin, William. *A Prophet with Honor: The Billy Graham Story* (Updated Edition). Zondervan, 2018.

Massie, Milton. "Naming Sin: A Response to the Killing of George Floyd" Cru. Accessed July 14, 2020. https://www.cru.org/us/en/communities/inner-city/media/naming-sin.html.

Matthews, Arthur. "Graham Scores at Notre Dame." *Christianity Today*, June 3, 1977.

McIntire, Carl. *The Rise of the Tyrant: Controlled Economy Vs. Private Enterprise*. Henry Ford Estate Collection. Christian Beacon Press, 1945.

McIntire, Carl. *Twentieth Century Reformation*. Christian Beacon Press, 1946.

Melnik, Glen. "Awake Thou That Sleepest or Who Are You Sleeping With?" *Sojourners*, September 1, 1971. https://sojo.net/magazine/fall-1971/awake-thou-sleepest-or-who-are-you-sleeping.

Merritt, Jonathan, "In 2008, I read a book that shattered many of my assumptions about God, faith, and what it means to follow Jesus. It was called 'Rich Christians in an Age of Hunger' by Ron Sider," Twitter, April 30, 2019, 11:24 p.m., https://twitter.com/JonathanMerritt/status/1123246756257587201

Miller, Emily. "Christian Author Jen Hatmaker on the 'Moxie' It Takes to Get Your Books Banned." *Sojourners*, August 7, 2017. https://sojo.net/articles/christian-author-jen-hatmaker-moxie-it-takes-get-your-books-banned.

———. "Evangelical Leaders Gather at Wheaton to Discuss Future of the Movement in Trump Era." *Sojourners*, April 17, 2018. https://sojo.net/articles/evangelical-leaders-gather-wheaton-discuss-future-movement-trump-era.

Miller, Steven. *Billy Graham and the Rise of the Republican South. Politics and Culture in Modern America.* University of Pennsylvania Press, Incorporated, 2011.

Miller, Steven Patrick. *The Age of Evangelicalism: America's Born-Again Years.* Oxford University Press, 2014.

Milliken, Bill. *So Long Sweet Jesus: A Street Worker's Spiritual Odyssey.* Prometheus Press, 1973.

Moberg, David. *The Great Reversal: Reconciling Evangelism and Social Concern.* Wipf & Stock Publishers, 2007.

Mollenkott, Virginia Ramey. "Women and the Bible." *Sojourners*, February 1, 1976. https://sojo.net/magazine/february-1976/women-and-bible.

Mollenkott, Virginia Ramey, and Richard Mouw. "Gay Marriage: Broken or Blessed? Two Evangelical Views." Interview by Krista Tippett, August 3, 2006. https://onbeing.org/programs/

richard-mouw-and-virginia-ramey-mollenkott-gay-marriage-broken-or-blessed-two-evangelical-views.

Moore, Russell. "The Evangelical Conscience: Still Uneasy After All These Years," September 17, 2003. https://www.russellmoore.com/2003/09/17/the-evangelical-conscience-still-uneasy-after-all-these-years.

———. "My colleague David Platt and I enjoyed being with Dr. and Mrs. Ronald Sider. Dr. Sider's writings on hunger influenced both of us.," Instagram, January 21, 2016. https://www.instagram.com/p/BA0rDEQTMWS.

Moore, Russell. *The Kingdom of Christ: The New Evangelical Perspective.* Crossway, 2004.

———. "My Top 10 Books of 2016," December 6, 2016. https://www.russell-moore.com/2016/12/06/top-10-books-2016.

Morley, Andrew. "Statement on Ending Racial Injustice." World Vision, June 11, 2020. https://www.wvi.org/newsroom/statement-ending-racial-injustice.

Mouw, Richard. "Weaving a Coherent Pattern of Discipleship." Christian Century, 1975.

Mouw, Richard, and Nathaniel Frank. What Do We Really Think About Homosexuality? Interview by Neal Conan, March 21, 2007. https://www.npr.org/templates/story/story.php?storyId=9041745.

———. *Consulting the Faithful: What Christian Intellectuals Can Learn from Popular Religion.* Wm. B. Eerdmans Publishing, 1994.

———. "Political Evangelism." *Sojourners,* May 1, 1973. https://sojo.net/magazine/may-june-1973/political-evangelism.

———. *Praying at Burger King.* Wm. B. Eerdmans Publishing, 2007.

————. *Restless Faith: Holding Evangelical Beliefs in a World of Contested Labels.* Brazos Press, 2019.

————. "Sexual Politics." *Sojourners*, August 1, 1974. https://sojo.net/magazine/ august-september-1974/sexual-politics.

————. *The Smell of Sawdust: What Evangelicals Can Learn from Their Fundamentalist Heritage.* Zondervan, 2000.

————. *Uncommon Decency: Christian Civility in an Uncivil World.* InterVarsity Press, 2011.

————, and *Douglas A. Sweeney. The Suffering and Victorious Christ: Toward a More Compassionate Christology.* Baker Academic, 2013.

————. *Abraham Kuyper: A Short and Personal Introduction.* Eerdmans Publishing Company, 2011.

————. *Adventures in Evangelical Civility: A Lifelong Quest for Common Ground.* Baker Publishing Group, 2016.

————. *Political Evangelism.* Books on Demand, 1973.

————. *Politics and the Biblical Drama.* Eerdmans, 1976.

Mulligan, Joe. "Thomas Merton's Secular Journal." *Sojourners*, March 1, 1973. https://sojo.net/magazine/march-april-1973/ thomas-mertons-secular-journal.

Nation, Mark. *John Howard Yoder: Mennonite Patience, Evangelical Witness, Catholic Convictions.* Wm. B. Eerdmans Publishing, 2006.

"New Berkeley Liberation Program." *Right On*, July 1969.

Newport, Frank. "In U.S., Four in 10 Report Attending Church in Last Week." Gallup, December 14, 2013. https://news.gallup.com/poll/166613/four- report-attending-church-last-week.aspx.

Nichols, Stephen. *Jesus Made in America: A Cultural History from the Puritans to "The Passion of the Christ."* InterVarsity Press, 2008.

Noble, Alan. *Disruptive Witness: Speaking Truth in a Distracted Age.* InterVarsity Press, 2018.

Noll, Mark A. *The Scandal of the Evangelical Mind.* Wm. B. Eerdmans Publishing, 1994.

Nouwen, Henri. "Letting Go of All Things." *Sojourners,* May 1, 1979. https://sojo.net/magazine/may-1979/letting-go-all-things.

Sojourners. "November-December 1973," November 1, 1973. https://sojo.net/magazine/november-december-1973.

Ockenga, Harold. "The Challenge to the Christian Culture of the West." Fuller Theological Seminary, October 1, 1947. https://fullerstudio.fuller.edu/the-challenge-to-the-christian-culture-of-the-west-opening-convocation-october-1-1947.

Osielski, David. "Senator Mark Hatfield Advocates 'Power of Love.'" Wheaton Record 96, no. 14 (February 15, 1974). https://recollections.wheaton.edu/2018/03/senator-mark-hatfield-advocates-power-of-love.

Palma, Robert. "Theology and Political Action." *Sojourners,* April 1, 1974. https://sojo.net/magazine/april-1974/theology-and-political-action.

Palmer, Jack. "Evangelical Leaders Announce Immigration Table Launch." *Sojourners,* June 12, 2012. https://sojo.net/articles/evangelical-leaders-announce-immigration-table-launch.

Pannell, William. *My Friend, the Enemy.* Word Books, 1968.

Perkins, John. *Let Justice Roll Down.* Baker Publishing Group, 2006.

———. "A Declaration Revisited." *Sojourners,* September 1, 1976. https://sojo.net/magazine/september-1976/declaration-revisited.

———. "Stoning the Prophets." *Sojourners*, February 1, 1978. https://sojo.net/magazine/february-1978/stoning-prophets.

———. *The Civil Rights Movement 50 Years after MLK*. MLK 50 Conference: The Gospel Coalition, 2018. https://youtu.be/q8KVSjrUqHo.

———. "The Dividing Wall in America." *Sojourners*, February 1, 1976. https://sojo.net/magazine/february-1976/dividing-wall-america.

———. "The Reconciled Community in a World at War." *Sojourners*, July 1, 1977. https://sojo.net/magazine/july-1977/reconciled-community-world-war.

———. *With Justice for All*. Ventura, CA: Regal Books, 1982.

Pinnock, Clark H. "A Call for Liberation of North American Christians." *Sojourners*, September 1, 1976. https://sojo.net/magazine/september-1976/call-liberation-north-american-christians.

———. "An Evangelical Theology of Human Liberation." *Sojourners*, February 1, 1976. https://sojo.net/magazine/february-1976/evangelical-theology-human-liberation.

———. "An Evangelical Theology of Human Liberation, Part II." *Sojourners*, March 1, 1976. https://sojo.net/magazine/march-1976/evangelical-theology-human-liberation-part-ii.

———. "Charismatic Renewal for the Radical Church." *Sojourners*, February 1, 1975. https://sojo.net/magazine/february-1975/charismatic-renewal-radical-church.

———. "Fruits Worthy of Repentance." *Sojourners*, December 1, 1977. https://sojo.net/magazine/december-1977/fruits-worthy-repentance.

———. "The Christian Revolution." *Sojourners*, September 1, 1971. https://sojo.net/magazine/fall-1971/christian-revolution.

Plowman, Edward E. "Carrying the Cross in the U.S.S.R." *Christianity Today,* December 20, 1974.

———. "Seeds of Schism: The Misery of Missouri." *Christianity Today,* May 10, 1974.

Piper, John. "World Hunger and Us," Desiring God, November 1, 1981, https:// www.desiringgod.org/messages/world-hunger-and-us.

Prior, Karen Swallow. *Fierce Convictions: The Extraordinary Life of Hannah More? Poet, Reformer, Abolitionist.* Thomas Nelson, 2014.

"Protestant Sects: 'The Body' Loses Its Earthly Head." *Christianity Today,* June 29, 1979.

Putman, Janene Cates. "An Interview with Letha Dawson Scanzoni." *Christian Feminism Today* (blog), March 21, 2019. https://eewc.com/ an-interview-with-letha-dawson-scanzoni.

Quebedeaux, Richard. *The Worldly Evangelicals.* Harper & Row, 1978.

———. *The Young Evangelicals: Revolution in Orthodoxy.* Harper & Row, 1974.

Rah, Soong-Chan. *In Whose Image: The Emergence, Development, and Challenge of African-American Evangelicalism.* PhD diss.: Duke University, 2016.

Rees, Paul. "Will Bangkok Be a Watershed or a Washout?" *World Vision Magazine,* December 1972.

Reese, Boyd. "America's Empire." *Sojourners,* November 1, 1973. https://sojo. net/magazine/november-december-1973/americas-empire.

———. "The Structure of Power." *Sojourners,* January 1, 1974. https://sojo.net/ magazine/january-1974/structure-power.

InterVarsity. "Remembering Pioneers," May 10, 2002. https://intervarsity.org/ news/remembering-pioneers.

David Berg. "Revolution for Jesus." Accessed February 19, 2020. https://www. davidberg.org/mission/revolution-for-jesus.

Rhoads, Gladys., and Nancy Anderson. McIntire. Xulon Press, Incorporated, 2012.

Risher, Dee Dee. "A Clarion of Justice." *Sojourners*, January 1, 2005. https://sojo. net/magazine/january-2005/clarion-justice.

Rottenberg, Isaac. "A Skeptical Response to Social Concern." *Sojourners*, May 1, 1976. https://sojo.net/magazine/may-june-1976/ skeptical-response-social-concern.

Ruotsila, Markku. *Fighting Fundamentalist: Carl McIntire and the Politicization of American Fundamentalism*. Oxford University Press, 2016.

Sabath, Bob. "Emily Post and Richard Nixon Revisited." *Sojourners*, March 1, 1972. https://sojo.net/magazine/spring-1972/ emily-post-and-richard-nixon-revisited.

Salley, Columbus, and Ronald Behm. *Your God Is Too White*. InterVarsity Press, 1970.

Urbana Student Missions Conference. "Samuel Escobar." Accessed April 30, 2020. https://urbana.org/bio/samuel-escobar.

Scanzoni, L., and N. Hardesty. *All We're Meant to Be: A Biblical Approach to Women's Liberation*. Word Books, 1974.

Scanzoni, Letha. "The Feminists and the Bible." *Christianity Today*, February 2, 1973.

Scanzoni, Letha Dawson. "The Life and Ministry of Nancy A. Hardesty." *Christian Feminism Today* (blog), January 22, 2012. https://eewc.com/ life-ministry-nancy-hardesty.

Schaeffer, F.A. *The Francis A. Schaeffer Trilogy: The Three Essential Books in One Volume.* Crossway Books, 1990.

Sessions, David. "Liberal Christians Attack Obama Spiritual Adviser Jim Wallis over Gay Ad." *The Daily Beast,* May 10, 2011. https://www.thedailybeast.com/articles/2011/05/10/liberal-christians-attack-obama-spiritual-adviser-jim-wallis-over-gay-ad.

Sharon Gallagher. "11-10-78 Sharon Gallagher." Westmont College, November 10, 1978. In *Chapel Podcast.* MP3 audio. http://archive.org/details/podcast_chapel-1978-1979_11-10-78-sharon-gallagher_1000111066198.

Shook, Jill. "Vietnam Today." *Right On,* April 8, 1974.

Sider, Ron. *Across the Spectrum: Why Abortion Is a Social Justice Issue for All Evangelicals.* The Ethics and Religious Liberty Commission of the Southern Baptist Convention, 2016. https://erlc.com/resource-library/event-messages/across-the-spectrum-why-abortion-is-a-social-justice-issue-for-all-evangelicals.

———. *The Chicago Declaration.* Wipf & Stock Publishers, 2016.

———. "Ron Sider: Why I Am Voting for Hillary Clinton." *Christianity Today,* October 2016.

———. "History Shows Us Why Being Evangelical Matters." *Christianity Today,* November 21, 2016. https://www.christianitytoday.com/ct/2016/november-web-only/history-shows-us-why-being-evangelical-matters.html.

———. "History Shows Us Why Being Evangelical Matters." *Christianity Today,* November 26, 2016. https://www.christianitytoday.com/ct/2016/november-web-only/history-shows-us-why-being-evangelical-matters.html.

———. "An Evangelical Theology of Liberation." *In Perspectives on Evangelical Theology,* 117–34. Baker, 1979.

————. "Evangelism, Salvation and Social Justice: Definitions and Interrelationship." *International Review of Mission*, January 1, 1975, 251–67.

————. *Rich Christians in an Age of Hunger*. New York: Paulist Press, 1978.

————. "Ronald J. Sider to Stephen Charles Mott," November 14, 1972. Billy Graham Center Archives.

————. *The Scandal of Evangelical Politics: Why Are Christians Missing the Chance to Really Change the World?* Baker Publishing Group, 2008.

————. "Tragedy, Tradition, and Opportunity in the Homosexuality Debate." *Christianity Today*, November 18, 2014. https://www.christianitytoday. com/ct/2014/november-web-only/ron-sider-tragedy-tradition-and-opportunity-in-homosexuality.html.

————. "What Should Be the Shape of the Evangelical Political Involvement in the 80's?," March 20, 1981. Folder "1981." ESA Archives.

Asian American Christian Collaborative. "Signed by Friends of the Asian American Community." Accessed April 8, 2020. https://asianamerican-christiancollaborative.com/signed-by-friends.

Singer, Charles. *A Theological Interpretation of American History*. International Library of Philosophy and Theology. Craig Press, 1964.

Skinner, Tom. *How Black Is The Gospel: A Decisive And Truthful Message for Today's Revolution*. Skinner Leadership Institute, 1970.

————. "The U.S. Racial Crisis and World Evangelism." Urbana Student Missions Conference, 1970. https://urbana.org/message/us-racial-crisis-and-world-evangelism.

Smedes, Lewis. *Sex for Christians: The Limits and Liberties of Sexual Living*. Eerdmans, 1976.

Smith Samuel. "'The Spiritual Danger of Trump:' New Book Asks Evangelicals to Rethink Their Vote in 2020," accessed July 13, 2020, https://www.christianpost.com/news/the-spiritual-danger-of-trump-new-book-asks-evangelicals-to-rethink-their-vote-in-2020.html.

Smith, Timothy. *Revivalism and Social Reform: American Protestantism on the Eve of the Civil War.* Wipf & Stock Publishers, 2004.

CNN. "Sojourners Presidential Forum," June 4, 2007. http://transcripts.cnn.com/TRANSCRIPTS/0706/04/sitroom.03.html.

Baptist Press. "Southern Baptist Leaders Issue Joint Statement on the Death of George Floyd." Accessed July 14, 2020. http://www.bpnews.net/54877/southern-baptist-leaders-issue-joint-statement-on-the-death-of-george-floyd.

Stafford, Tim. "Ron Sider's Unsetting Crusade." *Christianity Today,* April 27, 1992.

Stanton, Elizabeth Cady, Susan Brownell Anthony, and Matilda Joslyn Gage, *History of Woman Suffrage* (Susan B. Anthony, 1889).

Asian American Christian Collaborative. "Statement on Anti-Asian Racism in the Time of COVID-19." Accessed April 8, 2020. https://asianamerican-christiancollaborative.com/covid19statement.

Stedman, Ray, and Charles Peter Wagner. "Should the Church Be a Melting Pot?" *Christianity Today,* August 18, 1978.

Steensland, Brian, and Philip Goff. *The New Evangelical Social Engagement.* OUP USA, 2014.

Steinberg, Neil. "Trump v. Jesus: Christians Can't Follow Both." Chicago Sun-Times, October 10, 2019. https://chicago.suntimes.com/columnists/2019/10/10/20908102/trump-jesus-christians-evangelicals-religion-jim-wallis-steinberg.

Steinbuch, Yaron. "Black Lives Matter Co-Founder Describes Herself as 'Trained Marxist.'" *New York Post*, June 25, 2020. https://nypost. com/2020/06/25/blm-co-founder-describes-herself-as-trained-marxist.

Stewart, James Brewer. *Holy Warriors: The Abolitionists and American Slavery.* Rev. ed. New York: Hill and Wang, 1976.

Stott, John. "The Lausanne Covenant: An Exposition and Commentary by John Stott (LOP 3)." *Lausanne Movement*, February 13, 1978. https://www. lausanne.org/content/lop/lop-3.

Stott, John. "The Conservative Radical." *Sojourners*, November 1, 1973. https:// sojo.net/magazine/november-december-1973/conservative-radical.

Stringfellow, William. "Technocracy and the Human Witness." *Sojourners*, November 1, 1976. https://sojo.net/magazine/november-1976/ technocracy-and-human-witness.

Swartz, David. *Moral Minority: The Evangelical Left in an Age of Conservatism.* University of Pennsylvania Press, 2012.

"The Last Word on 1967." *Christianity Today,* December 22, 1967.

Lausanne Movement. "The Lausanne Covenant," August 1, 1974. https://www. lausanne.org/content/covenant/lausanne-covenant.

"The Purpose of the Person." *Christianity Today,* December 21, 1973.

Urban Project - Los Angeles. "The Three R's." Accessed May 2, 2020. http:// www.urbanprojectinternational.com/contact.

Thompson, Chad. *Loving Homosexuals as Jesus Would: A Fresh Christian Approach.* Brazos Press, 2004.

Thornwell, John Henley. *The Rights and Duties of Masters: A Sermon Preached at the Dedication of a Church Erected in Charleston, S. C., for the Benefit and*

Instruction of the Coloured Population. Birney Anti-Slavery Collection. Press of Walker & James, 1850.

Tidball, Derek. "The New Gospel of Community." *Third Way,* April 1980.

"Timothy Smith and the Recovery of the Nazarene Vision." *Holiness Today,* March 1999.

Tippett, Krista. Khaled Abou El Fadl, Richard J. Mouw, and Yossi Klein Halevi — The Power of Fundamentalism, April 18, 2002. https://onbeing.org/programs/khaled-abou-el-fadl-richard-j-mouw-and-yossi-klein-halevi-the-power-of-fundamentalism.

Jemar Tisby, "While it is tempting to create new declarations . . . never overlook the saints of the past who have already done this work . . .To address contemporary debates, sometimes it is not necessary to re-litigate but simply to re-discover," Twitter, September 10, 2018, 5:39 p.m. https://twitter.com/JemarTisby/status/1039267078447001607.

Toland, Eugene, Thomas Fenton, and McCulloch Lawrence. "World Justice and Peace: A Radical Analysis for American Christians." *The Other Side,* 1976.

Torrey, R.A. *The Fundamentals - A Testimony to the Truth.* Vol. 3. Rio, WI: AGES Software, 2000.

Turner, John. *Bill Bright and Campus Crusade for Christ: The Renewal of Evangelicalism in Postwar America.* University of North Carolina Press, 2009.

Uwan Ekemini. "Some of y'all are decolonizing your faith to the point that you're decolonizing your way out of the faith," Twitter, July 2, 2020, 9:32 a.m. https://twitter.com/sista_theology/status/1278682997320036354.

Wallis, Jim. *Agenda for Biblical People.* Harper & Row, 1976.

————. *Faith Works: Lessons from the Life of an Activist Preacher.* Random House Publishing Group, 2000.

————. *Revive Us Again: A Sojourner's Story.* Abingdon Press, 1983.

————. *The Great Awakening: Seven Ways to Change the World.* HarperCollins, 2009.

————. *The New Radical.* Lion Publishing, 1983.

————. "A Conversation with Young Evangelicals." *Sojourners,* January 1, 1975. https://sojo.net/magazine/january-1975/conversation-young-evangelicals.

————. "Biblical Politics." *Sojourners,* April 1, 1974. https://sojo.net/magazine/april-1974/biblical-politics.

————. "Building Up the Commonlife." *Sojourners,* April 1, 1976. https://sojo.net/magazine/april-1976/building-commonlife.

————. "Idols Closer to Home." *Sojourners,* May 1, 1979. https://sojo.net/magazine/may-1979/idols-closer-home.

————. "Interview: Carl Henry on Evangelical Identity." *Sojourners,* April 1, 1976. https://sojo.net/magazine/april-1976/interview-carl-henry-evangelical-identity.

————. "Interview with Samuel Escobar." *Sojourners,* September 1, 1976. https://sojo.net/magazine/september-1976/interview-samuel-escobar.

————. "Liberation and Conformity." *Sojourners,* September 1, 1976. https://sojo.net/magazine/september-1976/liberation-and-conformity.

————. "Many to Belief, but Few to Obedience." *Sojourners,* March 1, 1976. https://sojo.net/magazine/march-1976/many-belief-few-obedience.

————. "Post-American Christianity." *Sojourners*, September 1, 1971. https://sojo.net/magazine/fall-1971/post-american-christianity.

————. "The Boston Affirmations." *Sojourners*, February 1, 1976. https://sojo.net/magazine/february-1976/boston-affirmations.

————. "The Economy of Christian Fellowship." *Sojourners*, October 1, 1978. https://sojo.net/magazine/october-1978/economy-christian-fellowship.

————. "The Move to Washington, D.C." *Sojourners*, August 1, 1975. https://sojo.net/magazine/august-september-1975/move-washington-dc.

————. "The New Community." *Sojourners*, September 1, 1973. https://sojo.net/magazine/september-october-1973/new-community.

————. "The New Regime." *Sojourners*, October 1, 1974. https://sojo.net/magazine/october-1974/new-regime.

————. "What Is the People's Christian Coalition." *Sojourners*, September 1, 1972. https://sojo.net/magazine/fall-1972/what-peoples-christian-coalition.

Wear, Michael. *Reclaiming Hope: Lessons Learned in the Obama White House About the Future of Faith in America* (Thomas Nelson, 2017).

Webber, Robert. *Evangelicals on the Canterbury Trail.* Church Publishing, Inc., 1985.

Weddle, Kendra, and Jann Aldredge-Clanton. *Building Bridges: Letha Dawson Scanzoni and Friends.* Wipf & Stock Publishers, 2018.

Wells, David. *No Place for Truth: Or Whatever Happened to Evangelical Theology?* Wm. B. Eerdmans Publishing, 1994.

Black Lives Matter. "What We Believe." Accessed July 14, 2020. https://blacklivesmatter.com/what-we-believe.

"Will 'Radical' Christianity Have Any Effect on the American Church?" *Christian Post,* September 17, 2010. https://www.christianpost.com/news/will-radical-christianity-have-any-effect-on-the-american-church.html.

"William E. Pannell." Fuller. Accessed April 28, 2020. https://www.fuller.edu/faculty/william-e-pannell.

Williams, Derek. "The Weakness of Evangelical Ethics." *Third Way,* January 13, 1977.

Wilson, Wendy. "Southern Baptist ERLC's Russell Moore Collaborating with Christians Who Promote Wealth Redistribution, Amnesty for Illegal Immigrants." *Tennessee Star,* September 12, 2017. https://tennesseestar.com/2017/09/12/southern-baptist-erlcs-russell-moore-collaborating-with-christians-who-promote-wealth-redistribution-amnesty-for-illegal-immigrants.

Wilson-Hartgrove, Jonathan. "John Alexander: Soul Friend I Never Knew." *Jonathan Wilson-Hartgrove* (blog), July 24, 2012. https://www.patheos.com/blogs/jonathanwilsonhartgrove/2012/07/john-alexander-soul-friend-i-never-knew.

Wink, Walter. "Unmasking the Powers." *Sojourners,* October 1, 1978. https://sojo.net/magazine/october-1978/unmasking-powers.

Winthrop, John. "A Model of Christian Charity." The Winthrop Society, 1630. https://www.winthropsociety.com/doc_charity.php.

Wise, Ted. *Jason Questions a Jesus Freak* (An interview from Ted Wise). Interview by Jason Cronn, September 13, 1997. https://www.pbc.org/messages/jason-questions-a-jesus-freak-an-interview.

Wooten, James. "Nixon Hears War Called a 'Sin.'" *The New York Times,* February 2, 1973, sec. Archives. https://www.nytimes.com/1973/02/02/archives/nixon-hears-war-called-a-sin.html.

Yoder, John Howard. "Living the Disarmed Life." *Sojourners,* May 1, 1977. https://sojo.net/magazine/may-1977/living-disarmed-life.

————. "The Biblical Mandate." *Sojourners,* April 1, 1974. https://sojo.net/magazine/april-1974/biblical-mandate.

————. *The Politics of Jesus.* Eerdmans, 1972.

For more information about

Jon Harris
and
Social Justice Goes to Church
please visit:

www.worldviewconversation.com

For more information about
AMBASSADOR INTERNATIONAL
please visit:

www.ambassador-international.com
@AmbassadorIntl
www.facebook.com/AmbassadorIntl

If you enjoyed this book, please consider leaving us a review on
Amazon, Goodreads, or our website.